European Soccer Leagues 2019

Shane Stay

EUROPEAN
SOCCER LEAGUES
2019

Everything You Need to Know
About the 2019/20 Season

Meyer & Meyer Sport

British Library Cataloguing in Publication Data
A catalogue record for this book is available from the British Library

European Soccer Leagues 2019
Maidenhead: Meyer & Meyer Sport (UK) Ltd., 2019
ISBN: 978-1-78255-175-1

© 2019 by Meyer & Meyer Sport (UK) Ltd.
Aachen, Auckland, Beirut, Cairo, Cape Town, Dubai, Hägendorf, Hong Kong, Indianapolis, Manila, New Delhi, Singapore, Sydney, Tehran, Vienna

Credits
Cover and interior design: Annika Naas
Layout: Zerosoft
Cover and interior photos: © dpa, © AdobeStock
Managing editor: Elizabeth Evans

Member of the World Sports Publishers' Association (WSPA) www.w-s-p-a.org
Printed by Books International
ISBN: 978-1-78255-175-1
Email: info@m-m-sports.com
www.thesportspublisher.com

CONTENTS

INTRODUCTION

With few exceptions, every top player from around the world winds up in Europe. And eventually Asia. And eventually the Middle East. And eventually the United States. But in their prime, every player worth a grain of salt wants a shot at Europe. This has been the way for many generations. It really started to escalate in the 1980s when South American players such as Maradona, Junior, and Careca found their way to the continent. As a result, it started to feel like this was the thing to do. Before them, a few like Pelé held back. Yet others made a leap for European greatness, but it hadn't quite opened up as much. There were plenty of players making the trip to Europe, but not in the great numbers that we see today. In fact, right now, it might be difficult for a TMZ-esque reporter to walk into a popular Brazilian airport and not see a player—wearing headphones and sports gear—either departing for Europe or returning from it. The 80s and 90s were gateway decades for South Americans, along with other players representing North America, Africa, and Asia; the floodgates were definitely open. By this time, globalization of soccer was really in full swing, and Europe was the elite place to be—a trend that has continued to this day.

The enthusiasm of the fans, the money, and the quality of play in countries like England, Germany, Spain, and Italy are second to none. These countires are the main destinations for elite talent. Reaching back in time, there are legendary players who defined the game, such as Bobby Charlton, Alfredo Di Stefano, Ferenc Puskas, George Best, Eusebio, Johan Cruyff, Paul Breitner, Michel Platini, Bryan Robson, Ruud Gullit, Roberto Baggio, and

Zinedine Zidane. The history of club soccer within these nations is vast, historic, and, at times, overwhelming, which is what distinguishes these places. Today, the talent flourishes as players continue to compete at the highest level, leaving a legacy that provides a playground for the best soccer in world; players like Cristiano Ronaldo, Kylian Mbappé, Luka Modric, Lionel Messi, Neymar, Dele Alli, Mohamed Salah, Thomas Muller, and many more. Because of past players' greatness, this new generation of talent has something special to strive for.

This book reviews the top European leagues, with some additional information on other teams and leagues. Sit back and enjoy the journey—the 2019-20 European Club season will be a good one.

ENGLAND–PREMIER LEAGUE

A Look Back: 2018-19

Top Players: Danny Welbeck, Mesut Özil, Mohamed Salah, Firmino, Fabinho, Marcus Rashford, Jesse Lingard, Paul Pogba, Kevin De Bruyne, Fernandinho, Raheem Sterling, David Silva, Sergio Aguero, Eden Hazard, Willian, Olivier Giroud, Pedro, Harry Kane, Jan Vertonghen, and Dele Alli.

MVP: Mohamed Salah.

The Teams
Manchester City
Liverpool
Arsenal
Tottenham Hotspur
Chelsea
AFC Bournemouth
Wolverhampton Wanderers
Manchester United
Watford
Leicester City
Everton
Burnley
Brighton & Hove Albion
Crystal Palace
West Ham United
Southampton
Fulham
Huddersfield Town
Newcastle United
Cardiff City

These were the teams from 2018-19 season. Going into 2019-20, there will likely be a rumbling in the standings. When teams want to win, and when teams strive to win, anything can happen… that's the beauty of each new season.

Top 5 Teams
Arsenal
Liverpool
Manchester United
Manchester City
Chelsea

ARSENAL

Twitter: @Arsenal
Founded in 1886
FA Cup: 13
FA Community Shield: 15
League Champions: 13
European Cup and UEFA Champions League: 0
UEFA Super Cup: 0

Known For
Strong attendance
Very passionate fans
Exciting games
Elite talent
Thierry Henry
Danny Welbeck
Mesut Özil
Aaron Ramsey

A BRIEF TEAM HISTORY

Legendary coach: Herbert Chapman, from 1925-34.

Stan Kroenke—the current owner—is reportedly not a fan favorite; oddly enough, this is the same Stan Kroenke who is unpopular with St. Louis fans for moving the NFL franchise, the St. Louis Rams, to Los Angeles. Kroenke is majority owner; also in the ownership mix is Alisher Usmanov, a billionaire from Uzbekistan. The arrangement between the two has an interesting backstory. From 2018, Tariq Panja of *The New York Times* wrote: "LONDON—The Russian tycoon Alisher Usmanov agreed on Tuesday to sell his 30 percent stake in Arsenal to the club's majority owner, the American billionaire E. Stanley Kroenke, an agreement that would end years of acrimony and values the English Premier League team at $2.3 billion.

"Mr. Kroenke and Mr. Usmanov spent years fighting for supremacy at Arsenal, buying up shares whenever they became available, and the deal clears the way for Mr. Kroenke to take the club private, an action that Mr. Usmanov had long blocked by refusing to sell his shares.

"Mr. Kroenke, whose family also owns several American sports franchises, including the Los Angeles Rams and the Denver Nuggets, gained the upper hand in July 2011, leaving Mr. Usmanov to do little more than complain from the sidelines or seethe privately in the luxury skybox he maintains at Arsenal's stadium.

"Mr. Usmanov accepted an offer of 550 million pounds in cash, or about $712 million, giving Mr. Kroenke more than the 90 percent stake required to purchase the remaining shares in the club, said Mr. Kroenke's investment company, KSE."1

In the coaching department, Arsenal is a team that is rebuilding from previous years. Though successful by comparison with lesser clubs around the continent, fans were looking for higher, loftier accomplishments and it was thought that maybe Arsene Wenger needed to be replaced. Wenger coached Arsenal for an amazingly long time: 1996 to 2018! With his departure, the team is rallying behind coach Unai Emery and a not-so-popular American owner, Stan Kroenke. (Kroenke can't catch a break.)

FACTS ABOUT THEIR CITY

London—one the world's most vibrant cities—hosts a number of pro soccer teams, including the elite Arsenal, the renowned Tottenham, the powerful Chelsea, the every-ready West Ham, and the club with maybe the coolest name in world soccer, Crystal Palace. Supporters of the Gunners are known as the Gooners, a group that strongly supports its team with a loudness rarely found elsewhere.

WHERE THE TEAM IS TODAY— TACTICS AND STRATEGIES

A lot is expected of Arsenal, and each year it seems to be a team in the mix, on the verge of something great.

Tactics and strategies: keep things upbeat and continue pushing the pace.

The Gunners play a skillful, upbeat, and determined style of game. It's a team that pushes the pace, using possession with a purpose to keep opponents off-balance and fans happy. Likely operating out of a 4-2-3-1, the Gunners have midfield contributions from the likes of Lucas Torreira, Granit Xhaka, and Mesut Özil to keep things dynamic and moving forward. In the high pace arena of the Premier League, Arsenal is ready for any challenge. A team that is solid in its approach, its one that will continue to thrive from the legacy Arsene Wenger left behind.

UNAI EMERY—A BRIEF COACHING PORTRAIT

Unai Emery—who was born in Spain—began coaching Arsenal in 2018. As a former midfielder who played for a handful of teams, he racked up the most games with Toledo in Spain. As a coach, he recently finished up with Paris Saint-Germain before taking the Arsenal job. Will Emery be able to sustain the different style of play in the Premier League? This is a question posed by many as he takes on the new season.

KEY PLAYERS AND THEIR CHARACTERISTICS

Danny Welbeck, Mesut Özil, and Aaron Ramsey

Danny Welbeck—born in 1990 in England—is a talented forward who's been racking up playing time with England's national side since 2011. Prior to joining Arsenal, Welbeck spent time with Sunderland, Preston North End, and Manchester

United. He's got speed and good ability on the ball. Keep an eye out for Welbeck creating shots for Arsenal up front.

Mesut Özil—a talented midfielder from Germany—has great touch on the ball, coupled with intuitive vision, whose passes tend to keep the flow going in a positive forward direction. Equipped with the World Cup title from 2014, Özil adds much-needed experience to Arsenal's quest for the FA Cup.

Aaron Ramsey—a versatile midfielder from Wales—has played a ton of games with the Gunners while also tallying up some playing time with Cardiff City and Nottingham Forest. The almost 30-year-old still has some good years left for Arsenal.

Overall Player Rating:
Danny Welbeck: 9.1
Mesut Özil: 9.4-9.6
Aaron Ramsey: 9

KEY PLAYER STATS

(Total career goals with this club)

	Games Played	Goals
Danny Welbeck	88	16
Mesut Özil	164	32
Aaron Ramsey	260	40

WHAT TO WATCH FOR ON TV—HOW MESSI, NEYMAR, RONALDO, AND OTHERS PLAY

Arsenal is a club with strong talent coming from practically every angle. Plenty of soccer fans know that Arsenal can bewilder opponents and stop them in their tracks. In fact, most fans would agree with this. By recruiting from abroad and developing players within its training academy, the club is able to attain this level of supremacy.

From the 2018-19 campaign, Arsenal had a number of players at its disposal, including the goalkeeping talent of Petr Cech, Bernd Leno, and David Ospina; the forward play of Pierre-Emerick Aubameyang, Joel Campbell, Alexandre Lacazette, Eddie Nketiah, Lucas Perez, Danny Welbeck; with the versatile midfield play of Mohamed Elneny, Matteo Guendouzi, Alex Iwobi, Ainsley Maitland-Niles, Henrikh Mkhitaryan, Mesut Özil, Aaron Ramsey, Lucas Torreira, and Granit Xhaka; with the defensive options of Hector Bellerin, Calum Chambers, Rob Holdin, Carl Jenkinson, Sead Kolasinac, Laurent Koscielny, Stephan Lichtsteiner, Konstantinos Mavropanos, Nacho Monreal, Shkodran Mustafi, and Lokratis Papastathopoulos.

There is a high level of production value from Mesut Özil and Aaron Ramsey in midfield. These two will be called upon to guide the team forward with skillful interplay, smart passing choices, and instrumental organization throughout the attack.

Emile Smith-Rowe is a young midfielder to keep an eye on. He is likely to make a splash with the first team.

As for veteran regulars, Arsenal is equipped and ready to go. Stephan Lichtsteiner—a defender from Switzerland—adds experience and steadiness on the outside of defense. You can't go wrong with contributions from the Costa Rican star, Joel Campbell, a crafty dribbler and creator, easily one of CONCACAF's best. With Danny Welbeck up top, making runs, creating space for teammates, Arsenal is a contender for the FA Cup, along with being one of the best on the continent.

WHAT ARE THEIR CHANCES OF WINNING THE FA CUP THIS YEAR?

It's a team that will definitely be in the mix.

Overall Team Ranking: 9.1

LIVERPOOL

Twitter: @LFC
Founded in 1892
FA Cup: 7
FA Community Shield: 15
League Champions: 18
European Cup and UEFA Champions League: 6
UEFA Super Cup: 3

Known For
Strong attendance
Very passionate fans
Exciting games
Long history of high-quality soccer
Elite talent
Bill Shankly
John Aldridge
Ray Houghton
Alan Hansen
Ian Rush
John Barnes
Steve Nicol
Robbie Fowler

Michael Owen
Jamie Carragher
Steven Gerrard
Fernando Torres
Luis Suarez
Philippe Coutinho
Mohamed Salah

A BRIEF TEAM HISTORY

From 1892 to present, with so many championships and accomplishments, it's hard to categorize Liverpool without dedicating a complete book, the size of an encyclopedia, to one of the giants of European soccer, with Bill Shankly—the great coach—front and center. Just a few stellar names from Liverpool's storied history include: John Aldridge, Ray Houghton, Alan Hansen, Ian Rush, John Harkes, Steve Nicol, Robbie Fowler, Michael Owen, Jamie Carragher, Steven Gerrard, Fernando Torres, Luis Suarez, Philippe Coutinho, Mohamed Salah.

FACTS ABOUT THEIR CITY

Liverpool—home of The Beatles—is situated in western England, not far from Manchester and Sheffield, with easy access to Northern Ireland and Ireland by way of the Irish Sea. Traditionally, Liverpool has been an industrial city—one that, over time, has adored its soccer team. Anfield—which holds a little over 54,000—has become one of the best known, and revered, stadiums in the world.

WHERE THE TEAM IS TODAY— TACTICS AND STRATEGIES

German coach Jürgen Klopp—often seen wearing stylish glasses—has been implementing his idea of how Liverpool should play. Kevin Draper of *The New York Times* elaborated on some of Klopp's approach: "The birth of the new Liverpool may have been Oct. 8, 2015, the day F.S.G. announced the hiring of Klopp, the former Borussia Dortmund manager. In less than three years, Klopp has become the exuberant, backslapping and hugging face of the club. His aggressive gegenpressing, or counterpressing, system is the key to Liverpool's ruthless attack, and it can be a pleasure to watch—provided you're not supporting the team being subjected to it.

"But Klopp also has brought a focus to Liverpool's transfer targets. With the help of Michael Edwards, the former head of analytics who has risen to become Liverpool's sporting director, he has built a team capable of playing the way he wants it to play, and of challenging its more moneyed rivals."[2] With that, Liverpool is certainly a team to reckon with in the Premeire League and throughout Europe.

Tactics and strategies: If it ain't broke, don't fix it.

Keep the squad in place and keep the momentum going in a positive direction. Liverpool is at the top of its game. Is there room for improvement? Sure, but things are going well, so why make any big changes to playing strategy at this point?

JÜRGEN KLOPP—A BRIEF COACHING PORTRAIT

Jürgen Klopp—born in 1967 in Stuttgart, West Germany—began coaching at Liverpool in 2015. He has plenty of experience under his belt having played with Mainz 05, amassing a little over 300 games from 1990 to 2001. Following his playing career, he ended up coaching Mainz 05, then Borussia Dortmund, followed by Liverpool.

KEY PLAYERS AND THEIR CHARACTERISTICS

Mohamed Salah, James Milner, Firmino, and Fabinho

Mohamed Salah—a star attacker from Egypt—has catapulted onto the international scene with explosive runs down the wing, a knack for dribbling around the box, and an eye for goals. Some players are game-changers, and Salah is one of them. Like Shevchenko, Denilson, and Robben, get the ball to Mo's feet, and something interesting is bound to happen.

James Milner provides steadiness and experience. As a longtime veteran game-manager, Milner is a timely asset for the club.

Firmino—the Brazilian attacker—will provide good skill up top, setting up teammates, creating opportunities for himself, while drawing defenders his way, which, in turn, should open things up for his teammates. He's a valuable asset in terms of bringing everything together. A good threat up top, Firmino, who has over 100 appearances with Liverpool, is a player who will be orchestrating the attack this season, and certainly one to watch.

Fabinho—a Brazilian with a handful of caps for his country and relatively new to Liverpool—should have an active year helping with defense and providing structure for the squad.

Overall Player Rating:
Mohamed Salah: 9.9
James Milner: 8.9
Firmino: 9.5
Fabinho: 9.4

KEY PLAYER STATS

(Total career goals with this club)

	Games Played	Goals
Mohamed Salah	71	51
James Milner	125	17
Firmino	135	48
Fabinho	25	1

WHAT TO WATCH FOR ON TV—HOW MESSI, NEYMAR, RONALDO, AND OTHERS PLAY

Probably operating out of a 4-2-3-1, Liverpool employs smart attacking soccer, crisp passing, high tempo on both sides of the ball, and a strong work rate from players.

You can't go wrong with Salah creating danger in the opposition's end. Georginio Wijnaldum and Virgil van Dijk add a solid presence, leaving Liverpool in a strong position to consistently win games over the long stretch of a season.

Some of the forwards from the 2018-19 season included Roberto Firmino, Danny Ings, Sadio Mane, Divock Origi, Mohamed Salah, Xherdan Shaqiri, Dominic Solanke, Daniel Sturridge, and Ben Woodburn; a few defenders available included Nathaniel Clyne, Virgil van Dijk, Trent Alexander-Arnold, Joe Gomez, Ragnar Klavan, Dejan Lovren, Joel Matip, Alberto Moreno, Connor Randall, and Andrew Robertson; the midfield options included Allan, Pedro Chirivella, Marko Grujic, Jordan Henderson, Naby Keita, Ryan Kent, Adam Lallana, Lazar Markovic, James Milner, Sheyi Ojo, Alex Oxlade-Chamberlain, Harry Wilson, Fabinho, and Georginio Wijnaldum. The goalies available were Loris Karius, Simon Mignolet, and Danny Ward.

Will Daniel Sturridge be around? That's a good question, and something to watch as the season progresses.

Should this group stay intact, it's a good pool for Klopp to work with. He's a coach with passion, one who can bring players together. As Lothar Matthaus pointed out in *FourFourTwo* (Issue 292, October 2018): "It's not just Pep Guardiola who makes players better; Klopp does, too. He's also a motivator, and not just with his words. When Liverpool score and he jumps around or runs to the players, that's not acting—it's how he feels inside. Players feel he's one of them. He's like a second father for the young players, talking with them and helping them."

Strong as usual, Liverpool is a definite contender for league supremacy and a team to watch for quality play up and down the field. Anfield will be rockin' each and every game.

WHAT ARE THEIR CHANCES OF WINNING THE FA CUP THIS YEAR?

Very good—top of the list.

Overall Team Ranking: 9.8

MANCHESTER UNITED

Twitter: @ManUtd
Founded in 1878
FA Cup: 12
FA Community Shield: 21
League Champions: 20
European Cup and UEFA Champions League: 3
UEFA Super Cup: 1

Known For
Strong attendance
Very passionate fans
Exciting games
A legendary program
Elite talent
George Best
Ryan Giggs
Eric Cantona
David Beckham
Wayne Rooney
Cristiano Ronaldo
Paul Scholes
Patrice Evra

Antonio Valencia
Marcus Rashford
Jesse Lingard

A BRIEF TEAM HISTORY

A legendary coach: Alex Ferguson

The Busby "babes" and George Best and Ryan Giggs and where to start? Manchester United, like Liverpool, are so completely overwhelmingly successful, with generation after generation of top-level talent and players from the UK and around the world, that it's hard to quantify them without a book that's potentially 5,036 pages long. Who can forget Bobby Charlton, Nobby Stiles, Bryan Robson, Mark Hughes, Jesper Olsen, David Beckham, Eric Cantona, Ruud van Nistelrooy, Cristiano Ronaldo, Wayne Rooney, and Edwin van der Sar? These are just a handful of great players who have represented United over the years, and there are plenty more to come.

FACTS ABOUT THEIR CITY

Manchester—which sits close to Liverpool on the west side of England—is traditionally an industrial city, known for producing cotton and various war-time supplies during WWII.

It notoriously sports two of the world's most famous clubs: Manchester United and Manchester City. Of course.

A little music: The Smiths came formed in Manchester back in the early 1980s.

Food: Good luck! It is England after all!

As for beer, that's another story. Locals have many interesting options, some of which include Marble Brewery, BlackJack Brewery, and Six O'Clock Beer Company.

WHERE THE TEAM IS TODAY— TACTICS AND STRATEGIES

This is not your Manchester United squad of 2007, however it's a good one. Likely operating out of a 4-3-3 or 4-2-3-1, José Mourinho has turned some drama into a show of sustainability from a group of players eager to keep United in top contention.

Tactics and strategies: build on last season and find harmony.

Some forwards at Mourinho's disposal during the 2018-19 season were Romelu Lukaku, Anthony Martial, Marcus Rashford, Alexis Sanchez; midfielders included Marouane Fellaini, Fred, Ander Herrera, Jesse Lingard, Juan Mata, Nemanja Matic, Scott McTominay, Andreas Pereira, Paul Pogba, and Ashley Young; defenders consisted of Eric Bailly, Cameron Borthwick-Jackson, Diogo Dalot, Matteo Darmian, Timothy Fosu-Mensah, Phil Jones, Victor Lindelof, Marcos Rojo, Luke Shaw, Chris Smalling, Axel Tuanzebe, Antonio Valencia; and the goalies included David de Gea, Lee Grant, Joel Pereira, and Sergio Romero.

Should this group stay together, it's a club that has a great deal of proving to do. It has to prove that it's the best in England.

On the plus side, United has the skillful play of Marcus Rashford, Fred, Jesse Lingard, and Paul Pogba, which should help galvanize productive scoring chances.

When it comes to United, there's always going to be high-level passing. The passes are smart, well-placed, and full of energy. Finding on-field harmony through team chemistry is a key goal for United this season. It will depend on the capability and talent of the players, certainly, and with a little time, Manchester United can get back to dominating the Premier League.

JOSÉ MOURINHO—A BRIEF COACHING PORTRAIT

José Mourinho—a talented coach originally from Portugal—took over the Manchester United gig in 2016. Prior to stepping into one of the greatest clubs in soccer world history, he had the privilege of leading a handful of other sides, including Real Madrid, Inter Milan, and Chelsea. Known for interesting news conferences, Mourinho, like it or not, has been part of some building drama around Manchester which may prove even more exciting down the road. Manchester United has been striving to be great again. Essentially, as long as United finds itself out of first place, drama will be around the corner. Fans are up in arms, the media jumps all over it, and the coach is left with an overwhelming challenge. Mourinho is definitely ready for it.

KEY PLAYERS AND
THEIR CHARACTERISTICS

Marcus Rashford, Jesse Lingard, Paul Pogba, Fred, and Antonio Valencia

Marcus Rashford adds speed to the attack, along with good runs in and around the box, an ability to put the ball in the back of the net, and a good sense of unselfish passing for teammates.

Jesse Lingard, one of England's new generation of stars, will be in full effect, operating out of the midfield with the hopes of bringing Manchester United back to greatness and number one in the standings. Lingard's been on loan with a number of teams, including Leicester City, Birmingham City, Brighton & Hove Albion, and Derby County. Along with his experience, while also representing the Three Lions, Lingard will be expected to bring in the results United fans are looking for.

Paul Pogba—the man who had a popular 2018 World Cup video diary—will be leading things from the center of midfield, getting in on tackles and creating opportunities for teammates on the field. Critics say Pogba is overrated, though his supporters (and Pogba!) would disagree. Regardless, the French midfielder has a lot of experience to draw on as a leader on the squad.

Fred—born in 1993—gets things going in the midfield, accelerating the pace of play with dynamic movement. He gained playing experience with Internacional—of Porte Alegre, Brazil (way down south)—along with Shakhtar Donetsk before landing in Manchester. Additionally, he's been pulling in time with Brazil since 2014. Keep an eye on the 5'7" Brazilian for exciting play this year and down the road.

Antonio Valencia—the pride of Ecuador—is a longtime member of Manchester United, keeping things steady on the outside. He is an athletic, strong, and almost indestructible midfielder; though because he was born in 1985, he may be approaching retirement soon. Too soon to call him the future coach of Ecuador? Time will tell.

Overall Player Rating:
Marcus Rashford: 9.3
Jesse Lingard: 9.3
Paul Pogba: 9
Fred: 9.1
Antonio Valencia: 8.8-9

KEY PLAYER STATS

(Total career goals with this club)

	Games Played	Goals
Marcus Rashford	108	27
Jesse Lingard	110	17
Paul Pogba	92	24
Fred	17	1
Antonia Valencia	240	17

WHAT TO WATCH FOR ON TV—HOW MESSI, NEYMAR, RONALDO, AND OTHERS PLAY

Under José Mourinho, United can provide massive threats—in the form of Marcus Rashford—into open space, while midfielders Paul Pogba and Jesse Lingard offer constructive play to build off of. Essentially, Pogba and Lingard can create space for themselves by dribbling, while they also orchestrate passes throughout the field which creates space for teammates. Pogba might be wanting a trade, and it will be interesting to see what happens. The base of defense is strengthened with Chris Smalling's aerial prowess by clearing out crosses and keeping things orderly.

You can always count on at least one goal from United, brisk passing when in possession—and thoughtful possession at that. The team has players with a knack for outplaying the opposition at any given moment. To reflect on tactics and strategies, in order to build on last season, team chemistry will be important for United. If it can do this then it should be in a good place.

Old Trafford, the legendary stadium, will feature, as usual, one of the greatest clubs comprised of the best talent, operating at a super-fast pace.

WHAT ARE THEIR CHANCES OF WINNING THE FA CUP THIS YEAR?

Not good, not bad. Given that it's Manchester United, the chances are always good.

Overall Team Ranking: 9.1

MANCHESTER CITY

Twitter: @ManCity
Founded in 1894
FA Cup: 5
FA Community Shield: 5
League Champions: 5
European Cup and UEFA Champions League: 0
UEFA Super Cup: 0

Known For
Strong attendance
Very passionate fans
Exciting games
Elite talent
Pep Guardiola
Carlos Tevez
Sergio Aguero
Kevin De Bruyne
Fernandinho
Raheem Sterling
David Silva

A BRIEF TEAM HISTORY

Manchester City has been on a roll of late. After the close of the 2018 Premier League season, City, after playing so well, was in unchartered territory. For starters, regardimg Manchester City's magical 2018 run: "City became the first club in English top-tier history to post 100 points," as summarized by Joshua Robinson of *The Wall Street Journal*.[3] It was an amazing accomplishment, one that Pep Guardiola—the wise world class, possession-oriented coach—directed from the sidelines. But that wasn't it, as Robinson further explained: "City's list of broken records this season goes on longer than City's wage bill, from scoring the most goals in Premier League history (106) to the longest winning streak (18 games), to the largest championship margin (19 points). On top of all that, they did it in style."[4]

Can this be repeated? How can a team be expected to surpass or even meet, yet again, such results? Manchester City is a team that may not surpass its own greatness, but its one expected to continue with greatness, with an eye on stacking its trophy case. With so much talent on the field, and in the coaching department, City has been making history of late, cementing the club's legendary status for the ages.

FACTS ABOUT THEIR CITY

Sometimes Manchester United and Manchester City can overwhelm the senses, obstructing other interesting facets of the city. Manchester has a lot of firsts. Evidently, the first free public library—Chetham's Library—began in Manchester in 1653. Manchester is known as the world's first industrial city. In fact, in 1830, the world's first passenger train station was built in, you guessed it, Manchester. The Manchester "Baby" was an early computer assembled in this great city of industry. Food? There's a lot too. For Asian cuisine, Curry Mile is the place to be, with over 70 Asian restaurants in very close proximity. The University of Manchester can brag of 25 Nobel Prize Winners connected to its school.

Now back to Shaun Wright-Phillips, Carlos Tevez, Kevin De Bruyne, Sergio Aguero, David Silva, and Pep Guardiola.

WHERE THE TEAM IS TODAY— TACTICS AND STRATEGIES

Likely using a 4-3-3, Manchester City has the defensive luxury of evenly pressing the ball, which, in the best case scenario, will cause turnovers. In this case, City will begin to overwhelm its opponent—usually a befuddled group of 10 men running about in front of an anxious goalie—with extremely well-crafted possession.

Tactics and strategies: good possession play from defenders is important for continued success.

Defensively, City is well-suited for any opponent with athleticism, organization and fluid possession. The latter tends to be a key element with any team led by Guardiola; in other words, keeping the ball away from one's opponent is often the best defense, and good possession always starts with defenders. From the 2018-19 season, the following options were available to Guardiola: Tosin Adarabioyo, Danilo, Jason Denayer, Vincent

Kompany, Aymeric Laporte, Eliaquim Mangala, Benjamin Mendy, Nicolas Otamendi, John Stones, and Kyle Walker. These players—should they remain with City throughout the season—are vital components for success. Keep an eye on their contributions to possession as they orchestrate everything from the back.

PEP GUARDIOLA—A BRIEF COACHING PORTRAIT

Pep Guardiola—the Spanish phenom of a coach who led Barcelona to Champions League titles in 2009 and 2011—is leading the cause for City, after arriving from a jaunt in Bayern Munich. Pep's approach is geared around possession, and his methods have paid off as Manchester City enjoyed one of its best years in 2017-18.

KEY PLAYERS AND THEIR CHARACTERISTICS

Kevin De Bruyne, Fernandinho, Raheem Sterling, and David Silva

The highly skilled and technically sound **Kevin De Bruyne** is an asset for City moving forward. De Bruyne has done well with Belgium, helping to raise his team to new heights, and he continues to be a preeminent attacking player in Europe.

Fernandinho—born in 1985 in Brazil—played with Atletico Paranaense (from Brazil) and Shakhtar Donetsk (from the

Ukraine) before joining Manchester City in 2013. The defensive midfielder has plenty of experience with Brazil's national team since 2011. *World Soccer* magazine (September 2018) printed the following about Fernandinho's teammates: "The central defenders all have questions marks against them: Vincent Kompany is never far from an injury lay-off, John Stones is prone to lapses in concentration, Nicolas Otamendi lacks composure and Aymeric Laporte is not as robust as he should be." True, this is insight a year or so removed, yet, all the same, whether such criticism may or may not be true, these are just a few issues Fernandinho and teammates will likely be dealing with in the 2019-20 season.

Raheem Sterling—a regular with the Three Lions—is about as quick as can be, with darting speed, agility, and tricky moves around the box. One drawback might be his light weight, though his aforementioned agility and speed make up for it.

David Silva equals craft and guile. A great left-footer with thoughtful passes in the back of his mind, Silva adds a one-two punch from his lucrative experience with the Spanish national team.

Overall Player Rating:
Kevin De Bruyne: 9.5
Fernandinho: 9.2
Raheem Sterling: 9.1
David Silva: 9.4

KEY PLAYER STATS

(Total career goals with this club)

	Games Played	Goals
Kevin De Bruyne	115	23
Fernandinho	192	18
Raheem Sterling	128	48
David Silva	278	54

WHAT TO WATCH FOR ON TV—HOW MESSI, NEYMAR, RONALDO, AND OTHERS PLAY

From the 2018-19 season, Manchester City tormented opponents with the midfield and forward play of Kevin De Bruyne, Fernandinho, Bernardo Silva, David Silva, Riyad Mahrez, Sergio Aguero, Raheem Sterling, along with the availability of Fabian Delph, Brahim Diaz, Phil Foden, Aleix Garcia, Ikay Gundogan, Oleksandr Zinchenko, Gabriel Jesus, Lukas Nmecha, Patrick Roberts, and Leroy Sane. In goal, the options included Claudio Bravo, Ederson, and Joe Hart. From the point of view of Manchester City fans, it would be great if this core group remained as one. From the point of view of Southampton or Crystal Palace, maybe not so much.

In general, fans should expect some of the highest quality soccer in Premier League memory. Manchester City—guided by one of the best coaches in the world right now, the always brilliant, Guardiola—has turned into a record-setting squad for the ages, one that is trying to make history yet again.

WHAT ARE THEIR CHANCES OF WINNING THE FA CUP THIS YEAR?

Very high.

Overall Team Ranking: 9.8

CHELSEA

Twitter: @ChelseaFC
Founded in 1905
FA Cup: 8
FA Community Shield: 4
League Champions: 6
European Cup and UEFA Champions League: 1
UEFA Super Cup: 1

Known For
Strong attendance
Very passionate fans
Exciting games
Elite talent
Frank Lampard
Didier Drogba
Eden Hazard
Willian
Olivier Giroud
Pedro

A BRIEF TEAM HISTORY

The always talented Chelsea was founded in 1905, with eight FA Cups to its name, including one European Cup and a UEFA Super Cup to brag about as well. Going into the 2018-19 season, Maurizio Sarri—born in Italy—stepped in as coach after Antonio Conte—also born in Italy—was let go. Team owner, Roman Ambramovich, who's been with Chelsea since 2003, was undoubtedly weighing this decision, while also being concerned about his UK visa not going through. In 2018, *The New York Times* reported, "When Chelsea, the London soccer team, defeated Manchester United to win Britain's FA Cup 10 days ago, the club's billionaire Russian owner, Roman A. Abramovich, was nowhere to be seen among the celebrants, prompting speculation that the government was holding up his application for a visa extension."[5] Some may argue that getting a visa is more of a challenge than owning a soccer team.

Drama surrounded Chelsea during an important 2019 EFL Cup final that eventually went to a penalty shootout in favor of Manchester City. Chelsea's very expensive and sought-after goalie, Kepa, took center stage with coach Sarri, and people from around the world couldn't believe what they were seeing: Sarri called for Kepa to sub out, and Kepa refused to come off the field. Astounding. It was an eye-opener. Sarri marched off initially, as if he were leaving altogether, but then he came back in. Roger Gonzalez from *CBS Sports* wrote: "Just shocking. There is no other way to put it. Here he is, the world's most expensive goalkeeper undermining his coach to stay in the final. And this all comes after Chelsea's poor run of form to start 2019."[6]

As Chelsea moves forward, trying to recover from many low points in 2019, it's a program that has exuded excellence over time and has every intention of continuing that trend for years to come.

FACTS ABOUT THEIR CITY

Where you have London, you have Chelsea, and the River Thames is nearby. Chelsea's games are played at Stamford Bridge, in South West London. The stadium was originally built in 1876 (with renovations since), and it generally seats a little over 40,000. Fans have many options for beer before and after games; they might be enjoying a few drinks at The Phene. Also, famous chef Gordon Ramsay has a well-regarded restaurant in the area.

WHERE THE TEAM IS TODAY— TACTICS AND STRATEGIES

When you have players like Eden Hazard, Willian, Olivier Giroud, and Pedro, good things should follow. And that's where Chelsea is going into the 2019 season. On paper, with this lineup, Chelsea looks unstoppable.

The 2018-19 season featured many talented players. In goal Chelsea had the options of Willy Caballero, and Kepa Arrizabalaga; on defense there was Marcos Alonso, Ethan Ampadu, Cesar Azpilicueta, Gary Cahill, Andreas Christensen, David Luiz, Emerson Palmieri, Antonio Rudiger, Davide Zappacosta, Kurt Zouma; midfielders included Tiemoue

Bakayoko, Ross Barkley, Danny Drinkwater, Cesc Fabregas, Jorginho, N'Golo Kante, Ruben Loftus-Cheek, Victor Moses, Charles Musonda, Kyle Scott, and Willian; the forwards were Tammy Abraham, Michy Batshuayi, Olivier Giroud, Eden Hazard, Alvaro Morata, and Pedro (who is more of an outside midfielder).

Tactics and strategies: get back into good form, keep the locker room together, and listen to the coach.

Chelsea was certainly in turmoil during 2018-19; the tumultuous season got very interesting when Kepa refused to be subbed out by coach Sarri. Such an act will ignite drama with fans, media, and the locker room. All the talk was about drama. As a result, Chelsea needs to find its form again, avoid on-field dramatics (such as Kepa refusing to be subbed), and, it should go without saying, listen to its coach. What happened to listening to the coach? Kepa clearly had no intention of doing so. (Many people think that since players are paid so much these days they feel like they are in charge and don't need to listen to anyone. After all, in many cases, players are paid more than coaches so why should they be told what to do?) Whether it was a misunderstanding or not, the bottom line is that Chelsea was making headlines because of drama as opposed to dominating the Premier League. With a little work, it's a club that can definitely get back into top form.

Likely fielding a 4-3-3, Chelsea will keep up the pace and swarm opponents with a high-pressure defense. Under coach Sarri, the Italian wonder with attention to detail, it's a team possessing overwhelming talent that will be very hard to defeat.

MAURIZIO SARRI—A BRIEF COACHING PORTRAIT

Maurizio Sarri—who hails from Italy, was never a professional player, and spent much of his life as a banker—rose to coaching at the highest level by a most unexpected route. After work, he would go and coach amateur sides. This led up and up, to higher levels. He eventually reached the head coaching position at Napoli in Serie A—amazing. Rory Smith of *The New York Times* wrote about Sarri: "A 59-year-old Italian, he is the 13th managerial appointment of Roman Abramovich's impatient tenure at Stamford Bridge, and he is hardly the first to lack a garlanded playing career: of his predecessors, much the same could be said of José Mourinho, Andre Villas-Boas and Rafael Benítez.

"Sarri is, it is true, a little older than most of his peers: though hardly ancient by managerial standards, he had to wait for his chance among the elite. He was 55 when he first coached in Italy's top division, Serie A, with Empoli, and 56 when he was given a chance by a major team: Napoli, the team he had supported from afar as a child."[7]

Sarri is said to be an old-school chain smoker who would likely light up around the bench during games if it were allowed. His approach to coaching is known for being very organized, while he also wants his players to have fun, as he believes that players having fun will not get as tired. Getting players to have "fun" at this level is sometimes a tricky juggling act, as professional soccer demands results above all else. To juggle the strenuous expectations people put on teams and the ability to have fun playing is more complex than it sounds, and, if it's done right, a lot of credit should be given to the coach. This is another thought-provoking psychological edge that Sarri uses to his advantage, which, aligned with other strengths, is what makes him an exceptional, one might say legendary, coach.

KEY PLAYERS AND THEIR CHARACTERISTICS

Eden Hazard, Willian, Olivier Giroud, and Pedro

Eden Hazard—the Belgian dynamo—is a persistent attacking player who usually gives opponents fits out wide where he dazzles with dribbling skill, technique, explosiveness, and overall prowess on the ball. He's "too quick" and very shifty, and his change of direction often leaves defenders in the dust.

Willian, like Hazard, is very quick, shifty, and elusive, using change of direction to his advantage and to bewilder defenders. Trying to keep up with Willian's pace is hard to do; as he keeps defenders off-balance, Chelsea will have good luck in the scoring department.

Olivier Giroud—who hails from France—is a classical finisher. The recent World Cup champ of 2018 will be the recipient of Hazard's and Willian's creative work down the flanks. As a taller target player, Giroud can finish off crosses with his head and any other opportunities around the box. Will his consistency in the scoring department be as good as it should be? That's a question Chelsea fans will be asking throughout the season, and it's something Giroud has been criticized for in the past.

Anyone who's spent loads of time playing with Messi, Iniesta, and Xavi should have a good handle on how the game must be played. **Pedro** lends a hand with constructive ball possession, crafty skill, and game managing. He's a solid player to have out wide and brings a great deal of experience and expertise from his days with Barcelona and the Spanish national team.

Overall Player Rating:
Eden Hazard: 9.8-9.9
Willian: 9.8-9.9
Olivier Giroud: 9.1
Pedro: 9.2

KEY PLAYER STATS

(Total career goals with this club)

	Games Played	Goals
Eden Hazard	242	85
Willian	195	29
Olivier Giroud	38	5
Pedro	123	28

WHAT TO WATCH FOR ON TV—HOW MESSI, NEYMAR, RONALDO, AND OTHERS PLAY

Marching down the field with electric pace and shifty moves is the counterpunching combo of Hazard and Willian, top-tier talent that will give any team fits. Pedro has the organizational passing affect, while Giroud adds his all-encompassing scoring presence around the box. The balance of Hazard, Willian, and Pedro should, in theory, compliment Giroud's efforts up top to put goals away in bunches. Though, throughout his career, Giroud has been known for inconsistency in the scoring department. Is the high pace style of the Premier League too much for the Frenchman to handle? Does he need a league less demanding in its ways? While this might be a possibility, Giroud also may benefit from the fast pace, generating more goals this season. With the aforementioned combination of attacking stars in place, Giroud could have many tap-ins if he plays his cards right and situates himself in the right positions around the box.

Also keep an eye on Tiemoue Bakayoko, a midfielder from France who has experience playing with Monaco.

Christian Pulisic, the rising American talent, might make a name for himself in the Chelsea blue. He has the talent, he's done well with Borussia Dortmund, and there's a big chance he could be impactful as a midfielder in the Premier League.

Young up-and-coming talent: Ethan Ampadu, a defender from Wales.

Always expect a strong performance from Chelsea, with dazzling skill, up-tempo passing, strong runs downfield, plenty of opportunities around goal, and strong defense. Whether any of these departments are lacking throughout the year, or in any given game, it's a team that can make up for it with pure individual talent.

WHAT ARE THEIR CHANCES OF WINNING THE FA CUP THIS YEAR?

Good, bordering on decent. But don't bet the bank on it.

Overall Team Ranking: 9.3

TOTTENHAM

BONUS TEAM: *An Extra Top Fiver Not in the Top Five*

Twitter: @SpursOfficial
Founded in 1882
FA Cup: 8
FA Community Shield: 7
League Champions: 2
European Cup and UEFA Champions League: 0
UEFA Super Cup: 0

Known For
Passionate fans
High-quality players
FA Cup championships
Gary Lineker
Harry Kane
Dele Alli

A BRIEF TEAM HISTORY

Tottenham is one of those older "established" clubs from days of yore, having formed in 1882, even before the Ford Model T was released. Throughout its existence, Tottenham has done well in England, winning the FA Cup eight times.

Tottenham's new stadium goes by Tottenham Hotspur Stadium, which holds a little over 62,000 wild enthusiastic fans deadset on seeing their team achieve glory; without a doubt, London is rocking when Tottenham takes the field.

By the time Gary Lineker suited up with Tottenham, he was a Golden Boot winner from the 1986 World Cup. One of Tottenham's former midfielders, Luka Modric, won the Golden Ball at the 2018 World Cup. Harry Kane, a member of Tottenham during the 2018 World Cup, won the Golden Boot in Russia.

FACTS ABOUT THEIR CITY

London has hosted Tottenham, one of its legendary teams, since 1882. As London hosts many soccer teams, it's also England's capital city, and the largest city in the United Kingdom and Europe. Throughout the years, London has established itself as a centerpiece for historic events; in particular, it has hosted the Olympics in 1908, 1948, and 2012. Also, Wembley Stadium, where Tottenham has played many games, was host of the World Cup final in 1966 whereby England defeated West Germany 4-2 for the title.

WHERE THE TEAM IS TODAY—
TACTICS AND STRATEGIES

Tottenham will probably go with a 3-1-4-2 (essentially a 4-4-2) or possibly a 4-2-3-1.

Tactics and strategies: get the most out of Harry Kane and Dele Alli.

Tottenham fans will be counting on Harry Kane and Dele Alli to carry the team throughout the season, as they are critical factors for offensive success. If those two are playing well, the team is playing well. Also critical for success is the presence of Jan Vertonghen on the backline. The highly experienced Belgian should be instrumental in getting Tottenham on track for a successful campaign this season.

MAURICIO POCHETTINO—
A BRIEF COACHING PORTRAIT

Mauricio Pochettino—who has experience playing as a defender for the Argentinian national team—began coaching Tottenham in 2014. He also adds a touch of expertise from his time playing professionally with Newell's Old Boys, Espanyol, Paris Saint-Germain, and Bordeaux.

KEY PLAYERS AND
THEIR CHARACTERISTICS

Harry Kane, Jan Vertonghen, and Dele Alli

Harry Kane—the Golden Boot winner from the 2018 World Cup—is an athletic guy who puts his body between the ball and defender very well. He's not fast or necessarily quick, yet, by using his body effectively, he finds a way to assert his presence into advantageous positions around the field, which inevitably results in a good buildup in possession or an opportunity to score. He's a baller, plain and simple.

Jan Vertonghen—born in 1987—started his professional career with Ajax. He holds a tight fort on defense, and the Belgian star has World Cup experience.

Dele Alli—born in 1996—helped guide England to the semi-finals in the 2018 World Cup alongside teammate Harry Kane. Alli has formidable touch and thoughtful awareness on the ball, delivering a solid product on offense.

Overall Player Rating:
Harry Kane: 9.5
Jan Vertonghen: 8.8
Dele Alli: 9.1

KEY PLAYER STATS

(Total career goals with this club)

	Games Played	Goals
Harry Kane	178	125
Jan Vertonghen	209	5
Dele Alli	128	42

WHAT TO WATCH FOR ON TV—HOW MESSI, NEYMAR, RONALDO, AND OTHERS PLAY

From the 2018-19 season, the defenders included Toby Alderweireld, Serge Aurier, Cameron Carter-Vickers, Ben Davies, Juan Foyth, Danny Rose, Davinson Sanchez, Keiran Trippier, Jan Vertonghen, Kyle Walker-Peters; while the midfielders consisted of Dele Alli, Mousa Dembele, Eric Dier, Christian Eriksen, Erik Lamela, Lucas Moura, Georges-Kevin N'Koudou, Josh Onomah, Moussa Sissoko, Victor Wanyama, and Harry Winks; and the forwards included Vincent Janssen, Harry Kane, Fernando Llorente, and Son Heung-min. The goalkeeper options were Hugo Lloris, Paulo Gazzaniga, and Michel Vorm.

With experienced players such as Jan Vertonghen, Erik Lamela, and Harry Kane, Tottenham is looking to achieve big things this year, and is a team with the potential to win the FA Cup.

WHAT ARE THEIR CHANCES OF WINNING THE FA CUP THIS YEAR?

Pretty good. Tottenham will have to chase Liverpool and Manchester City yet again. Tottenham did very well last season. In terms of last season's standings, it was a team knocking on the door of first and second place, in line with Arsenal, Manchester United, and Chelsea.

Overall Team Ranking: 9.2

THE UNDERDOGS

Wolverhampton
Everton
Leicester City

WOLVERHAMPTON

Twitter: @Wolves
Founded in 1877
FA Cup: 4
FA Community Shield: 0
League Champions: 3
European Cup and UEFA Champions League: 0
UEFA Super Cup: 0

Known For
Strong history
Very passionate fans
Billy Wright
Steve Bull

A BRIEF TEAM HISTORY

Let's get to it: Wolverhampton formed in 1877. (That's along time ago! The up-and-coming league of Major League Soccer kicked off in 1996 and has a lot of catching up to do!) It's a club that's featured top-notch players such as Billy Wright and Steve Bull.

In the 1950s, Wolverhampton was one of the best in England and Europe. Since then, there have been some good times, but, by and large, it's been a team wandering in search of greatness.

Currently, a Chinese group has purchased the club, and many are optimistic about the future. Fans are hoping that some of the past magic of Steve Bull will emerge from today's players.

FACTS ABOUT THEIR CITY

Wolverhampton, essentially located in central England, has a population of around 259,900.

Have you ever wondered which was the first city in Britain to have automated traffic lights? It was Wolverhampton—back in 1927 "in Princes Square at the junction of Lichfield Street and Princess Street."[8]

Billy Wright, who was born in 1924, played 490 games for the Wanderers and represented the English national team with 105 caps.

WHERE THE TEAM IS TODAY— TACTICS AND STRATEGIES

There is a lot to think about these days in the Wolverhampton camp.

Tactics and strategies: Should Wolverhampton go with three defenders? Probably not.

With Wolverhampton taking the field, as was the case in the 2018-19 season, you might see a 3-4-3 or 3-4-1-2 or 3-4-2-1; the latter two are essentially a 3-4-3. Some may wonder whether a 3-4-3 is a bit like a 4-3-3, considering the option of a defensive center mid stepping back for defensive help. Whenever a team decides to go with three defenders, it seems like a risky, some may argue unorthodox, attempt at a formation (even with a center mid dropping back for support). Will this possibly hold the team back from its true potential? Should a new formation be tossed into the mix? Yes, and yes.

The great Brian Clough thought little of formations. Instead, he stressed that the important thing is how the players *play* (regardless of the formation). Essentially, that's what Wolverhampton—a program looking to get back on top—should be concerned with.

NUNO ESPIRITO SANTO— A BRIEF COACHING PORTRAIT

Nuno Espirito Santo—who was born on the islands of Sao Tome and Principe off the western coast of Africa—played goalie for several pro teams before turning to coaching. As a coach he's landed with Rio Ave (Portugal), Valencia (Spain), and Porto (Portugal). Now Santo has his sights set on making Wolverhampton great again.

KEY PLAYERS AND
THEIR CHARACTERISTICS

Rui Patricio, Conor Coady, and Ivan Cavaleiro

Rui Patricio, who likely many fans do not know, is a goalie from Portugal who played with Sporting CP before arriving at Wolverhampton. As an experienced keeper with the Portuguese national team, Patricio brings confidence and wisdom to the table. His acquisition comes across as a wise move by Wolverhampton to achieve top-level status again.

Conor Coady—born in 1993—is a defender originally from Liverpool, England. As captain of the Wanderers, Coady is positioned to lead from the back and guide the club to a phenomenal season.

Ivan Cavaleiro is an attacking player from Portugal—with experience on the Portuguese national team—looking to make a difference up top this season with a ton of goals.

Overall Player Rating:
Rui Patricio: 8.3
Conor Coady: 7.9
Ivan Cavaleiro: 7.8

KEY PLAYER STATS

(Total career goals with this club)

	Games Played	Goals
Rui Patricio	30	0
Conor Coady	153	1
Ivan Cavaleiro	93	17

WHAT TO WATCH FOR ON TV—HOW MESSI, NEYMAR, RONALDO, AND OTHERS PLAY

A few players seen in the 2018-19 season were Helder Costa, Adama Traore, and Raul Jimenez up top; Jonathan Castro, Romain Saiss, Joao Moutinho, and Matt Doherty at midfield; with Willy Boly, Conor Coady, and Ryan Bennett on defense. On its route to finding greatness, a good amount of English and Portuguese players joined the effort in Wolverhampton. Following modern trends, it was, in fact, an international effortwith other players coming from Ireland, Scotland, Belgium, France, Spain, Morocco, Mexico, and Brazil.

While Wolverhampton is trying to get back to where it used to be, many trials and tribulations should follow and to expect anything close to the recent success of Leicester City would be highly doubtful. With that said, Wolverhampton should be a team that is, slowly but surely, building success.

WHAT ARE THEIR CHANCES OF
WINNING THE FA CUP THIS YEAR?

Ricky Gervais, in his current shape today, has a better chance to play center forward for Manchester United.

Overall Team Ranking: 8.0

EVERTON

Twitter: @Everton
Founded in 1878
FA Cup: 5
FA Community Shield: 0
League Champions: 9
European Cup and UEFA Champions League: 0
UEFA Super Cup: 0

Known For
Strong attendance
Very passionate fans
Exciting games
Dixie Dean
Alan Ball
Trevor Steven
Graeme Sharp
Wayne Rooney

A BRIEF TEAM HISTORY

The Everton boys in blue and white, also known as "The Toffees" and "The Blues," have a long history and have boasted many talented players over the years, ranging from Dixie Dean, Alan Ball, Trevor Steven, Graeme Sharp, and Wayne Rooney. Dating back to 1878, Everton has attained five FA Cups and nine league championships.

FACTS ABOUT THEIR CITY

Liverpool isn't just the home of The Beatles. Many people outside of England might not know that Everton is based in Liverpool, home to the other well-known club: Liverpool. Back in 1989, Everton and Liverpool squared off in the FA Cup final in a legendary game in which Liverpool eventually won by a score of 3-2.

Everton's stadium is known as Goodison Park, which was built in 1892 and holds 39,572 people.

WHERE THE TEAM IS TODAY— TACTICS AND STRATEGIES

As was the case in the 2018-19 season, Everton was seen using a 4-4-1-1 or 4-2-3-1. Should this continue is yet to be seen in 2019-20. It's a team with strong attacking players, including Bernard, Gylfi Sigurosson, Theo Walcott, and Richarlison.

Tactics and strategies: keep a good rhythm throughout the season and capitalize on experienced players.

One challenge for Everton will be to keep these players in rhythm throughout the season, creating many chances to score. Easier said than done. Can Everton capitalize on the value its experienced players bring to the table, or should team chemistry be an issue? This is not yet known as Everton moves forward, seeking to improve on last season.

MARCO SILVA—A BRIEF COACHING PORTRAIT

Marco Silva—born in 1977—is a coach from Portugal looking to ignite a spark in Everton with the hope of winning the FA Cup. He's a relatively new coach with the club, and, based on his past coaching experience—rlatively short durations with other clubs— don't be surprised to see a change sometime soon.

KEY PLAYERS AND THEIR CHARACTERISTICS

Gylfi Sigurosson and Theo Walcott

Gylfi Sigurosson—an attacking midfielder from Iceland—has played with a few teams before his time with Everton, including Swansea City and Tottenham. Everton is counting on old Gylfi to establish a strong presence throughout the season and connect smart passes with teammates, drawing on his experience from Iceland's national team.

Theo Walcott is an experienced player with time spent at Southampton and Arsenal. As a speedy attacking player, one with a large amount of experience on England's national team, Walcott is a threat in attacking positions, and Everton is counting on him to create many scoring chances this season.

Overall Player Rating:
Gylfi Sigurosson: 9
Theo Walcott: 9.2

KEY PLAYER STATS

(Total career goals with this club)

	Games Played	Goals
Gylfi Sigurosson	62	17
Theo Walcott	48	7

WHAT TO WATCH FOR ON TV—HOW MESSI, NEYMAR, RONALDO, AND OTHERS PLAY

This 2019-20 season should be an exciting one for Everton. It's a team looking to expand on the experience it gained last year. The 2018-19 season saw Richarlison at forward; with attacking mid help from the Icelandic wonder Gylfi; in midfield there was Bernard the Brazilian out wide, Idrissa Gueye, Andre Gomes (who was on loan), and Theo Walcott; while defenders consisted of Lucas Digne, Yerry Mina, Michael Keane, and Seamus Coleman, with Jordan Pickford in the net. Should things change in Everton's lineup, it will still be a club with good potential in the attack and a well-equipped defense.

Will Everton live up to larger expectations by winning the FA Cup? It's possible, but don't count on it this year.

WHAT ARE THEIR CHANCES OF WINNING THE FA CUP THIS YEAR?

Hold your horses! Not great, not bad, but not great.

Overall Team Ranking: 8.0

LEICESTER CITY

Twitter: @LCFC
Founded in 1884
FA Cup: 0
FA Community Shield: 0
League Champions: 0
European Cup and UEFA Champions League: 0
UEFA Super Cup: 0

Known For
Strong attendance
Very passionate fans
Exciting games
Shaking up the Premier League with underdog victories
Claudio Ranieri
Jamie Vardy

A BRIEF TEAM HISTORY

Home games for Leicester City take place in King Power Stadium, which was built in 2002 and holds a little over 32,000 people. Leicester City has had four second-place finishes in the FA Cup, the last one being in 1969. 2016 was a big year for Leicester City. Led by the Italian coach Claudio Ranieri, the club took home a few honors, including "BBC Sports Personality Team of the Year Award," "BBC Sports Personality Coach of the Year Award," and "ESPN Team of the Year."

In 2018, an unfortunate incident occurred as the owner and chairman of Leicester City, Vichai Srivaddhanaprabha—who was originally from Thailand—died in a helicopter crash along with four companions following a game against West Ham.

FACTS ABOUT THEIR CITY

Leicester is located in central England with a population of around 329,000 people. Anyone visiting Leicester might want to check out Everards Brewery, which dates back to 1849.

WHERE THE TEAM IS TODAY—
TACTICS AND STRATEGIES

This season, Leicester will be a club eager to capitalize on success from the 2018-19 season. With the momentum it's had for the past few years, this is a team clearly on the rise, and it should be known that such a team is ready for bigger and better things. Its fan base is eager as well. The whole organization is doing what it can to stay ahead of the curve, and for now, things are looking good. All in all, would it be crazy to say Leicester has its eye on the European championship? Not at all. That's the type of team it is; the idea of shocking the world is something expected from Leicester at this point. Still, don't be surprised to see an all-out march to the UEFA Champions League final in the near future. On route to this goal, and to achieve Premeire League dominance, Leicester will likely use a 4-3-3 or a 4-2-3-1.

Tactics and strategies: stay consistent, use central players, involve defenders in the attack.

In order to escape from the rut of being a middle-of-the-road team, Leicester needs to attain a certain level of consistency. Easier said than done. Indeed, last season Leicester had highs and then lows, and by lows one would wonder if such a losing streak would've been accepted in the locker room of Liverpool or Manchester City. One must be thinking, "For God's sake, there's so much talent. How can it be winning one day and then losing to so-and-so the next?" Yet Leicester achieved such results. Not a good place to be if it's a team hungry for the UEFA Champions League title.

Use central players. Pretty simple. Yet, by using the middle positions more often, Leicester can then exploit the wings more effectively. This is key. This is not to say that Leicester never used central players, or, in fact, used them ineffectively—not at all. Though, any team stuck in the middle, so to speak, for large durations of time should be a team to take a step back and reanalyze its approach. Usually successful teams, that is to say, successful teams that win consistently, will use the central positions—the center mids—with great skill. Should Leicester improve in this regard, things will pick up dramatically.

Involve defenders in the attack. One way to take the Premier League by storm, yet again (though maybe a few years removed), is to get the defenders involved in the attack on a more regular basis. This is important, yet, in many cases, teams often neglect it. Leicester in particular has so many opportunities to throw outside defenders up, with instructions to shoot more often, or, at the very least, engage areas in and around the box with creative dribbling, while central defenders could, theoretically, engage themselves up field more often as well. Using one of the central defenders à la Franz Beckenbauer would be a positive; get players up front with constructive passing in mind. Any time an extra defender joins the attack with the intent of helping in possession, more passing lanes open up, and gaps in the defense begin to show the leads to better scoring opportunities. What did Sergio Busquets do when he sauntered into the attack? He wasn't Denilson, that's for sure. He became a simple wall pass for the other players. Give him the ball, and he'd give it right back. It was, and is, a brilliant tactic to keep the flow of possession going, and this type of play from a defender—on offense, that is—is crucial to render midfielders and forwards more options in the passing structure; it gets those players going, and they begin to play with more confidence. These are important points for Leicester—a highly talented team with potential through the roof—to consider on its path to Premier League dominance this season and the next.

BRENDAN RODGERS—
A BRIEF COACHING PORTRAIT

Before Brendan Rodgers was Claude Puel. As a coach, Puel—who was born in 1961 in France—brought experience from Southampton, Nice, Lyon, Lille, and Monaco. As a player, he spent what seems like most of his life with Monaco, playing an astounding 488 games with the French club.

Under his guidance, Puel had an opportunity to keep Leicester City going strong, and the fans were hoping for big results from the

Frenchman. However, things didn't turn out as Puel had expected. The current leader of the cause for Leicester City (a fine one at that) would be none other than Brendan Rodgers, who recently left the coaching position at Celtic (after much success). He previously led Liverpool as well. After a good run with Celtic up in the Scottish Premiership, Rodgers is excited about another go in the Premier League. Leicester City fans are all but panting over the prospects of this 2019-20 season, which should prove to be a brilliantly exciting one.

KEY PLAYERS AND
THEIR CHARACTERISTICS

Jamie Vardy, Kelechi Iheanacho, and Demarai Gray

Jamie Vardy, a forward with experience playing on the English national team, is a veteran with Leicester City looking to capitalize on a strong season. Born in 1987, Vardy is now in his thirties, and Leicester City should be counting on his leadership to guide the team in a positive direction.

Kelechi Iheanacho is a forward from Nigeria ready to build on his previous success with Leicester City and increase his goal tally.

Demarai Gray, typically found on the outside, has tallied up a good amount of experience with Leicester City, and this should serve the team well on its quest for the FA Cup this season.

Overall Player Rating:
Jamie Vardy: 8.6
Kelechi Iheanacho: 8.5
Demarai Gray: 8.5

KEY PLAYER STATS

(Total career goals with this club)

	Games Played	Goals
Jamie Vardy	236	98
Kelechi Iheanacho	50	4
Demarai Gray	105	8

WHAT TO WATCH FOR ON TV—HOW MESSI, NEYMAR, RONALDO, AND OTHERS PLAY

The sparkling play of Leicester City will be on full display this year. Jamie Vardy, Kelechi Iheanacho, and Demarai Gray—assuming they're injury free—should be going full throttle with an eye for goal, distributing the ball, setting up teammates, and, hopefully for the sake of Leicester fans, tucking away wins. It's a good-looking season for Leicester, and with a strong lineup, it's a team that can be in the hunt for the league's best record.

Keep an eye on whether Leicester can remain consistent, use central players, and involve defenders in the attack. These are vital components to success. The players are definitely capable of brilliance. Whether Leicester can deliver will be another story altogether.

WHAT ARE THEIR CHANCES OF WINNING THE FA CUP THIS YEAR?

You never know. It's a good club with a lot of tricks up its sleeve.

Overall Team Ranking: 8.9

GERMANY—
BUNDESLIGA

A Look Back: 2018-19

Top Players: Manuel Neuer, Robert Lewandowski, Joshua Kimmich, James Rodriguez, Thomas Muller, Julian Brandt, Kai Havertz, Kevin Volland, Charles Aranguiz, Lars Stindl, Raffael, Tobias Strobl, Thorgan Hazard, Mario Gotze, Marco Reus, Paco Alcacer, Maximilian Philipp, Jadon Sancho, Thomas Delaney, Timo Werner, Yussuf Poulsen, Diego Demme, Luka Jovic, Andrej Kramaric, Ishak Belfodil, Wout Weghorst, Jean-Philippe Mateta, Alassane Plea, Alfred Finnbogason, Ondrej Duda, Dodi Lukabakio, Max Kruse, and Willi Orban.

MVP: Robert Lewandowski. (Marco Reus and Timo Werner deserve an honorable mention as well.)

The Teams
Borussia Dortmund
Borussia Monchengladbach
Werder Bremen
Hertha Berlin
Bayern Munich
RB Leipzig
Mainz
VfL Wolfsburg
FC Augsburg
Nurnberg
TSG Hoffenheim
Eintracht Frankfurt
SC Freiburg
Schalke 04

Bayer Leverkusen
Hannover 96
Fortuna Düsseldorf
VfB Stuttgart

These were the teams from 2018-19 season. Going into 2019-20, there will likely be a rumbling in the standings. When teams want to win, and when teams strive to win, anything can happen… that's the beauty of each new season.

Top 5 Teams
Bayern Munich
Bayer 04 Leverkusen
Borussia Monchengladbach
Borussia Dortmund
RB Leipzig

BAYERN MUNICH

Twitter: @FCBayern
Founded in 1900
German Champions: 28
European Cup and UEFA Champions League: 5
UEFA Super Cup: 1

Known For
Strong attendance
Very passionate fans
Exciting games
Gerd Müller
Franz Beckenbauer
Paul Breitner
Karl-Heinz Rummenigge
Philipp Lahm
Bastian Schweinsteiger
Toni Kroos
Lothar Matthäus
Manuel Neuer
Franck Ribery
Arjen Robben
Thomas Müller

A BRIEF TEAM HISTORY

When it comes to excellence, one could successfully argue there is no greater presence in German soccer than Bayern Munich. It has won the German League 28 times and counting, with titles from smaller tournaments—DFB-Pokal, DFL-Supercup, and DFL-Ligapokal—along with European titles to boot, adding up like a seventh-grader's math homework.

Bayern flourished big time in the 1970s, with some of its most iconic players taking center stage around that time. This was a golden era for Bayern Munich as the club won the European Cup in three consecutive tournaments (1973-74, 1974-75, and 1975-76). Franz Beckenbauer, the elegant "queen on the chessboard," operating from defense, was captain from 1970-77.

The players that have roamed through the halls of Germany's finest club add up like an A list of the Bundesliga's who's who: Gerd Müller, Franz Beckenbauer, Paul Breitner, Karl-Heinz Rummenigge, and Lothar Matthäus, to name a few. In the modern era, the list of talent continues with Philipp Lahm, Bastian Schweinsteiger, Toni Kroos, Manuel Neuer, Franck Ribery, Arjen Robben, Robert Lewandowski, and Thomas Müller. There are so many other players worth mentioning that would require leasing out a bookstore worth of space.

But wait. As great as Bayern is, last season (that of 2018-19) left room for discussion after the team struggled, losing more than expected, and talk of coach Niko Kovac's departure was looming. Franck Ribery and Arjen Robben are growing older. These two have been absolutely critical to Bayern's success in recent years. As they are moving closer to retirement, Bayern has been in limbo somewhat. Though, as should be expected, Bayern will look to make drastic improvements for the 2019-20 season.

FACTS ABOUT THEIR CITY

Munich is the capital of Bavaria and is situated in the southern area of Germany, very close to Austria. Bayern Munich entertains (and usually annihilates) its opponents at Allianz Arena, which opened in 2005, and is known for its color-changing exterior. It's unique because all panels change color. While people can see this ongoing color show on the outside, the 75,000 fans are rocking on the inside. Karl-Heinz Rummenigge—a former Bayern Munich captain—still plays a role with the team as chairman of the executive board

WHERE THE TEAM IS TODAY— TACTICS AND STRATEGIES

It's automatically assumed that a team like Bayern will be successful. So what's the formula? What has worked? What hasn't worked? Typically, Bayern has been seen with a 4-3-3. And superior talent tends to help. In fact, superior talent trumps any formation. Aside from the 4-3-3, Bayern might use a 4-4-1-1 or possibly a 4-1-4-1. Perhaps the 4-3-3 would be best as the 4-3-3 has been used affectively by Bayern in its ability to pressure opponents on defense. The beauty of the 4-3-3 is that is makes the field smaller (defensively), as players can easily cover more ground on the field together, pressing the opponent and causing turnovers.

Tactics and strategies: keep the play flowing, implement new talent.

When a team like Bayern Munich is in the conversation, there isn't much advice to be given. Unless, of course, major blunders are occurring, which they aren't. Well, according to die-hard fans that want to see Bayern go undefeated each year, the 2018-19 season was a blunder of epic proportions. Though, generally speaking, if one were to compare Bayern to other teams from around the world, then the consensus would be that things are pretty good in Munich. The only thing holding Bayern back is Bayern. It's a team with so much talent that it's hard to think anything except that it can win the league outright for the next 10 years. (Unless Borussia Dortmund has something to say about it.) It's also easy to illustrate how Bayern—arguably the greatest German team in existence—can be considered as a strong contender for the Champions League title this time around, and easily for the next three to five years after that. But how can it achieve Bundesliga dominance while also posing a threat to the Champions League? After all, Bayern is in a transition period with relatively new players that were featured in 2018-19 such as Leon Goretzka, Serge Gnabry, and Kingsley Coman (somewhat new, anyway), but it's definitely a club flowing with time, keeping its lineup fresh as players like Ribery and Robben eventually reach the age of no return and move on or retire. The fans and front office recognize that Ribery and Robben can't hold on to their thirties forever and playing the role of "Roger Milla" can only go so far; this might be an attractive option, but it has its limits.

Quite simply, Bayern needs to keep the flow going. One big point of interest in this regard will be to implement new talent. In particular, Bayern needs to be out in front with the transition from Ribery and Robben to new, worthy, talent in those positions.

It's such a salient issue, and one Bayern fans would probably want to avoid. How can you replace Ribery and Robben? Quite simply, you can't. You can, but it won't be the same. These are two of the greatest outside talents the Bundesliga has welcomed. The next players up will have an enormous challenge to live up to the standard left by Ribery and Robben. Nonetheless, it's an interesting development to watch in the next few years.

NIKO KOVAC—A BRIEF COACHING PORTRAIT

Niko Kovac—a former Bayern Munich player in the early 2000s—was born in West Germany and eventually played with the Croatia's national team. Kovac has received quite a bit of criticism for his coaching time with Bayern. The 2018-19 season was not a huge success, and Bayern was chasing Borussia Dortmund instead of leading from a comfortable position. Kovac will be expected to turn this around, and soon. A lot of weight rests on his shoulders, and until he can guide the team to its potential, he will continue to feel the wrath of fans and critics alike.

KEY PLAYERS AND THEIR CHARACTERISTICS

Manuel Neuer, Robert Lewandowski, Joshua Kimmich, James Rodriguez, and Thomas Müller

Recently, **Manuel Neuer**—a World Cup champion with Germany—has dealt with criticism and a hand injury. A hand injury is significant for any player, especially a goalie. On

February 4, 2019, *The Washington Post* reported that Neuer, "has looked a shadow of his former self when he has played this season. Once touted by German pundits as the best goalkeeper in the world, it's no longer certain whether Neuer, 32, is even the best in the country."[9] Indeed Neuer has been one of the best goalies in modern soccer. As for what lies next. Only time will tell.

Robert Lewandowski—the Polish wonder—is a valuable striker to have on the field. Period. Lewandowski's ability to score is similar to Pele's simple chalkboard description of himself in the movie *Victory,* in which he explains to his teammates—played by Michael Caine, Osvaldo Ardiles, and others—how they just need to give him the ball, and he weaves his way downfield and scores. Minus the dribbling prowess, there's a similar vibe with Lewandowski; if you need a ball put in the back of the net, then look no further. If Lewandowski is on the field, then there will likely be goal. It's as simple as that. Will he dazzle you with dribbling around the box? No. Will he lace in a beautiful through-pass like Platini or Ronaldinho? Probably not. But it's more likely than the dribbling. However, what Lewandowski specializes in is finishing around goal with uncanny technique, accuracy, and intuitive instincts. As long as he's healthy and ready to go, Bayern is in a good position to succeed.

Joshua Kimmich—born in 1995—is younger German talent leading the way for Bayern Munich and the German national team. He is multitalented with a specialty in defensive help, making him a valuable presence for Bayern as he keeps things steady on the backline.

James Rodriguez—one of Colombia's finest—was caught up in a tax-fraud scheme during his time in Spain. No one's really surprised. News of that situation hit magazines, and whether it will affect his play on the field is yet unknown. The Colombian frontman is known for dazzling shots on goal, including the ability to knock down a flamboyant bicycle kick. He is thought of as one of the world's current elite players, which is why Bayern acquired him. Though, the tax issue is likely something Bayern officials prefer to leave in Spain. Will he stay with Bayern? Will he exit for Real Madrid, or yet another team? It's very possible for Rodriguez to depart Bayern for another option and such a move would not be surprising at all.

Thomas Müller has been effective as a starter, and coming off the bench and he should continue this role with Bayern this season. You can always count on his deft field awareness to create plays and finish around goal.

Overall Player Rating:
Robert Lewandowski: 9.8
Joshua Kimmich: 9.4
James Rodriguez: 9.5
Thomas Muller: 9.5

KEY PLAYER STATS

(Total career goals with this club)

	Games Played	Goals
Robert Lewandowski	155	127
Joshua Kimmich	109	9
James Rodriguez	42	14
Thomas Müller	314	110

WHAT TO WATCH FOR ON TV—HOW MESSI, NEYMAR, RONALDO, AND OTHERS PLAY

Robert Lewandowski, Joshua Kimmich, James Rodriguez, Franck Ribery, and Thomas Müller form a solid group that has tormented opponents with incredible team structure, consistency, and flair for years. Thiago, Rafinha, Jerome Boateng, David Alaba, Javi Martinez, and Mats Hummels have provided structure which in turn has provided Bayern with an elite platform to operate from.

Keep an eye on Arjen Robben and Franck Ribery, two of the best outside attackers in the Bundesliga, and arguably in the history of world soccer. Both players are getting older, and they might not be around for much longer. How effective will they be? This will definitely depend on injuries.

One player who is supposed to have a strong impact is the young Canadian, Alphonso Davies, who was traded from Vancouver Whitecaps with a lot of chatter and high expectations.

Entering the 2018-19 Bundesliga season, Bayern Munich enjoyed six, count them, six, titles in a row. Though, things weren't exactly flowing as anticipated. In fact, during the 2018-19 campaign, Bayern struggled a bit. On February 4, 2019, which was well into the season, *The Washington Post* reported: "Dortmund is already seven points clear this season and looks a far better bet for the title than Niko Kovac's disjointed team. Bayern hasn't been helped by injuries to Arjen Robben, Franck Ribery, James Rodriguez, Thiago Alcantara and goalkeeper Manuel Neuer, among others."[10]

When it's all said and done, the most salient issue might be a coaching change. An abrupt one at that might be in the works if Bayern doesn't get back to its dominating ways.

WHAT ARE THEIR CHANCES OF WINNING THE LEAGUE TITLE THIS YEAR?

Very, very high.

Overall Team Ranking: 9.4

BAYER 04 LEVERKUSEN

Twitter: @bayer04fussball @bayer04_en
Founded in 1904
German Champions: 0
European Cup and UEFA Champions League: 0
UEFA Super Cup: 0

Known For
Strong attendance
Very passionate fans
Exciting games
Nickname: Die Werkself
Stefan KieBling
Ulf Kirsten
Thomas Horster
Herbert Waas
Dimitar Berbatov
Lars Bender
Sven Bender
Julian Brandt
Kevin Volland

A BRIEF TEAM HISTORY

Call them "the team of runners-up," and you might not get out of the stadium alive. However, it seems to be a club obsessed with second-place finishes. Aside from winning the DFB-Pokal (1992-93), and UEFA Cup (1987-88), Bayer Leverkusen has come in second for a number of finishes including the Bundesliga (1996-97, 1998-99, 1999-2000, 2001-02, 2010-11), DFB-Pokal (2001-02, 2008-09), DFB-Supercup (1993), and UEFA Champions League (2001-02). Don't call them second best. But you might not have any other choice.

Michael Schade—team chairman—along with coach Peter Bosz, who hopped on board quite recently, are looking to change the team's second-place streak sometime very soon.

FACTS ABOUT THEIR CITY

BayArena hosts Leverkusen games. It's been around since 1958, with a few improvements along the way, and holds a little over 30,000 people. Leverkusen is a city located in the German state of North Rhine-Westphalia, which geographically rests in the beautiful northwest area of the country with close access to Belgium and the Netherlands.

WHERE THE TEAM IS TODAY—
TACTICS AND STRATEGIES

The 4-3-3 has provided success for Bayer in the past, and, should the club stay with it, good things will occur. The 4-3-3 allows for more defensive support as it enables the players to cover more areas of the field.

A few players involved in the 2018-19 season were Leon Bailey, Lucas Alario, Kevin Volland, Karim Bellarabi, Julian Brandt, Charles Aranguiz, Kai Havertz, Wendell, Lars Bender, Sven Bender, Jonathan Tah, Mitchell Weiser

Bayer was looking for someone who embodied German *fußball*, someone creative, dependable, focused, steady, smart, determined, polite, professional, arrogant, confident, cool. It turned out to be Julian Brandt—a coach's dream come true. He could handle the critics; in fact, he could keep them away with stellar play; that was the idea. One look at him, and you know he is a player who emobides everything a team wants.

Strength, vigor, and reliable describes what you get on defense with Sven Bender. Operating with craft and guile ahead of Sven was Charles Aranguiz.

Though, Bayer found itself wandering around eighth place at times. A far cry from where it thought it should be. Clearly things weren't going according to plan. Was it the formation? Was it the personnel? Was it bad luck? It was definitely a talented team not living up to its potential. Perhaps Bailey and Volland aren't top class. Perhaps the combination of Aranguiz and Brandt and Havertz is not a marriage made in heaven.

Tactics and strategies: improve consistency, along with more connectivity in possession play.

Generally speaking, while fans are ready to turn on coaching and players that aren't living up to their greatest strengths, each player is placed on the field to avoid an all-out mutiny. Outrage, perhaps even low-level mutiny, can arise from fans, writers, people that think they know more about the game than any one person is allowed to. But, for a club like Bayer, an all-out mutiny from different angles is probably not going to be a reality. An interesting point is that Bayer does not have the international, historic prestige that Real Madrid, Barcelona, AC Milan, and Manchester United do. Therefore, in somewhat of a paradox, when the Champions League trophy doesn't appear, this might be a reason why no one is outraged around Bayer. Are people upset? Sure. On the flipside, if Bayer produces a phenomenal Bundesliga season, which it should, then fans are content. This is partially one of the advantages Bayer has up its sleeve.

PETER BOSZ—A BRIEF COACHING PORTRAIT

Peter Bosz was born in 1963 in the Netherlands and played midfield with his national team and a number of professional sides, including Toulon and Feyenoord. Since 2000, he's had a hand in a number of coaching assignments, with recent stops at Ajax and Borussia Dortmund before landing with Bayer in 2018. With Bayer, he has an assortment of talent at his disposal, including Kevin Volland, Julian Brandt, and Sven Bender, and the pressure is on to deliver a winning season in steadfast form.

KEY PLAYERS AND
THEIR CHARACTERISTICS

Julian Brandt, Kai Havertz, Kevin Volland, and Charles Aranguiz

Julian Brandt—born in 1996—is one of Germany's rising stars. He took home a silver medal from the 2016 Olympics in Brazil in which Germany lost to Neymar and the hosts in penalty kicks. Brandt will likely have many more opportunities to represent Germany down the road. As for Bayer 04 Leverkusen, Brandt is the future. As an attacking midfielder, he possesses skill, knowledge, good rhythm and a will to win. A combination hard to find in most players.

Kai Havertz was born in 1999 in Aachen, Germany. The young midfielder already has more than 75 games with Bayer Leverkusen, and he's marching past 15 goals scored. He's a rising star to watch in the years to come.

Kevin Volland, born in 1992, is a versatile German forward and has played with the German national team. While he's not the fastest forward in the world, he has craft and guile, and he's alert around the box with a good finishing touch.

Charles Aranguiz has been with Chile's national team since 2009. Prior to joining Bayer Leverkusen, the Chilean midfielder was with Sport Club Internacional out of Porto Alegre, Brazil. He'll be found in the middle of the field distributing the ball hopefully turning this season around for Bayer.

Overall Player Rating:

Julian Brandt: 9.4

Kai Havertz: 8

Kevin Volland: 8.1

Charles Aranguiz: 8.1

KEY PLAYER STATS

(Total career goals with this club)

	Games Played	Goals
Julian Brandt	160	31
Kai Havertz	83	20
Kevin Volland	79	31
Charles Aranguiz	74	6

WHAT TO WATCH FOR ON TV—HOW MESSI, NEYMAR, RONALDO, AND OTHERS PLAY

The recent acquisition of Paulinho Henrique Sampaio Filho—a promising 5'9" Brazilian forward born in 2000—will be one to watch as he develops in the Bundesliga.

Julian Brandt, the versatile attacking midfielder, is a key figure in attack. Should Brandt find success in little moments throughout a game, so should Bayer in the wins column.

Leon Bailey, Lucas Alario, Kevin Volland, Charles Aranguiz, Karim Bellarabi, Sven Bender, and Lars Bender are a few players who will guide Bayer forward this season with swift, accurate passing and fluid team movement.

Bayer players seem to glide past opponents, whether it's passing or dribbling. Consistency is key for Bayer. Can it stay consistent? Can Brandt produce on a consistent basis? Can Volland match that? Time will tell as Bayer continues its quest to sit atop the standings in the Bundesliga.

WHAT ARE THEIR CHANCES OF WINNING THE LEAGUE TITLE THIS YEAR?

Pretty good.

Overall Team Ranking: 8.4

BORUSSIA MONCHENGLADBACH

Twitter: @borussia @borussia_en
Founded in 1900
German Champions: 5
European Cup and UEFA Champions League: 0
UEFA Super Cup: 0

Known For
Strong attendance
Passionate fans
Exciting games
A rivalry with 1. FC Köln
Hennes Weisweiler
Allan Simonsen
Dieter Hecking
Raffael
Lars Stindl

A BRIEF TEAM HISTORY

Borussia Monchengladbach won the Bundesliga during the good years on five occasions (1969-70, 1970-71, 1974-75, 1975-76, 1976-77). A featured forward during the 70s was Allan Simonsen (who also represented the Danish national team). It won the DFB-Pokal on three occasions (1959-60, 1972-73, 1994-95). As for the UEFA Cup, it took first place in 1974-75 and 1978-79. It took second-place in the 1976-77 European Cup, losing to Liverpool.

While Monchengladbach is a team that has drifted in and out of relevancy, it has remained in the race, always striving to get better.

FACTS ABOUT THEIR CITY

Monchengladbach, a city of around 260,000 people, is on the western border of Germany, near Dortmund, Düsseldorf, and Cologne. Beer? Try a drink from the brewery of Brauerei zum Stefanus. If you stop by Uwe Beer, just know that it's a hair salon.

WHERE THE TEAM IS TODAY— TACTICS AND STRATEGIES

Dieter Hecking has established players at his disposal, including Lars Stindl and Thorgan Hazard. The club hit its stride during the previous 2018-19 season and is looking for more success this time around. During 2019-20, it wouldn't be farfetched to see a 4-3-3 which brought the club good results last year.

Tactics and strategies: stay consistent, concentrate on flow of play, don't worry about scoring goals.

It's easy for critics or a coach to say, "stay consistent," but in Borussia Monchengladbach's case, it's a matter of seeing games out and cruising past weaker opponents. Often, it's easy to play at the level of the weaker team. A key to success for Borussia Monchengladbach will be to outplay weaker teams and remain at a high standard in those games. It's always tempting to let go and trade punches with a weaker team, but this is a trap which must be avoided.

One way to stay consistent is to concentrate on the flow of play. In other words, keep focused on possession. If Borussia Monchengladbach can outplay opponents in possession-oriented soccer, then it should do very well. In past years (2008-2011), Michael Bradley was brought in to help guide this flow. Tobias Strobl held the keys to midfield in 2018-19, and this season should follow a similar trend. With the help of Stindl and Hazard, possession play should be fluid and fun. If this happens, then goals should occur more frequently.

If Borussia Monchengladbach gets caught up in whether or not it's scoring enough, then there will be problems. Good possession soccer will lead to more scoring chances, and that's key. If the club keeps this in mind, then good things will come.

DIETER HECKING—A BRIEF COACHING PORTRAIT

Dieter Hecking was born in 1964 in West Germany and eventually played as a midfielder for a number of teams such as Borussia Monchengladbach (where he started his professional career) and Hannover 96. Hecking's job, simply, might just be to keep the critics at bay. There will be voices saying he needs to get Monchengladbach into the number one position, that he can't get his side in the number one position. Because no matter what, the coach gets the blame. They'll say he's a bad coach, that he has no idea even how to coach. As Hecking avoids the chatter, his main goal should be to keep his club focused on the task at hand: winning the Bundesliga. That's when the noise will stop, for a little bit anyway.

KEY PLAYERS AND THEIR CHARACTERISTICS

Lars Stindl, Raffael, Tobias Strobl, and Thorgan Hazard

Lars Stindl—born in 1988 in West Germany—is a forward with previous experience at Hannover 96 and Karlsruher SC. He's also spent time on Germany's national team. As captain of Monchengladbach, he's responsible for leading the team in the locker room with the added pressure of scoring goals. His team did well last year, and it's planning on riding that wave of momentum to an even better season in 2019-20. Although, fans and owners are expecting more from the team, and it's up to Stindl to deliver.

Raffael is a Brazilian-born forward who has played over 145 games for Monchengladbach, tormenting defenses with over 55 goals—though he might not be as relevant with the club much longer. He's entering his mid-thirties, and management will try to see how much more it can squeeze out of his bag of tricks, as he'll likely come off the bench as the "Roger Milla factor." During a 1-1 draw between Monchengladbach and SC Freiburg on March 15, 2019, it was announced that Raffael signed a new deal through 2020, so things will fall as they may after that.

Tobias Strobl can be found in midfield, orchestrating the attack with deft touch. He brings previous experience to the table from having played with TSG 1899 Hoffenheim, and 1. FC Köln. He has the responsibility of guiding the attack with possession-oriented soccer, and such a task will call upon his ability to consistently string passes together cohesively. If he can remain successful in this regard, it should be a winning season for the club.

Thorgan Hazard—the dynamic offensive talent from Belgium— will be counted on for surging attacks, assists, and plenty of goals this season. With over 130 games for Monchengladbach, Hazard is a force to be reckoned with out wide where he will continue to dazzle defenses with skill and quickness.

Overall Player Rating:
Lars Stindl: 8.3
Raffael: 8.4
Tobias Strobl: 8.5
Thorgan Hazard: 8.9

KEY PLAYER STATS

(Total career goals with this club)

	Games Played	Goals
Lars Stindl	111	27
Raffael	149	57
Tobias Strobl	48	0
Thorgan Hazard	169	31

WHAT TO WATCH FOR ON TV—HOW MESSI, NEYMAR, RONALDO, AND OTHERS PLAY

A couple things to watch for with Monchengladbach include finding a good rhythm, staying consistent, passing cohesively, and attacking quick down the wings.

For fans of yesterday, fans that have enjoyed the play of Raffael, just know that he might not be around for long. What trade value does he have as a Brazilian attacker in his mid-thirties? Considering his age, not much. Unless you consider trading him to India, Vietnam, or Turkey as being valuable. It will be interesting to see how he plays out. There still might be room for him within the squad, but you never know. He was a hell of a player, with a big impact on the team, which is why he was included as a Key Player, but all good things come to an end. Hopefully, for Monchengladbach fans, he has a few more years left.

Lars Stindl, Tobias Strobl, Thorgan Hazard should be playing well, with surging attacks and methodic passing. They'll be leading the team forward, and if things play out accordingly, Monchengladbach could be on route to a Bundesliga title.

WHAT ARE THEIR CHANCES OF WINNING THE LEAGUE TITLE THIS YEAR?

Not the best, but it's possible.

Overall Team Ranking: 8.9

BORUSSIA DORTMUND

Twitter: @BVB @BlackYellow
Founded in 1909
German Champions: 8
European Cup and UEFA Champions League: 1
UEFA Super Cup: 0

Known For
Strong attendance
Very passionate fans
Exciting games
Lucien Favre
Mario Götze
Marco Reus
Maximilian Philipp
Jadon Sancho
Thomas Delaney
Christian Pulisic

A BRIEF TEAM HISTORY

Borussia Dortmund has won the Bundesliga (German soccer championship) on eight occasions (1956, 1957, 1963, 1994-95, 1995-96, 2001-02, 2010-11, and 2011-12). In addition, it has won the DFB-Pokal on four occasions (1964-65, 1988-89, 2011-12, and 2016-17). It also won the DFL-Supercup on five occasions (1989, 1995, 1996, 2013, and 2014).

On the continent, Borussia Dortmund won the UEFA Champions League in 1996-97 by defeating Juventus in the final 3-1. It also won the European Cup Winners' Cup (AKA the UEFA Cup Winners' Cup) in 1965-66. (This competition lasted from 1960-1999.)

FACTS ABOUT THEIR CITY

Dortmund is a beautiful city founded in 882 AD and located in the western part of Germany. If you're in town, check out the Dortmunder Actien Brauerei brewery which dates back to 1868.

The stadium for Borussia Dortmund is called Westfalenstadion (AKA Signal Iduna Park), which opened in 1974. It's had a few renovations since then and holds a capacity of a little over 81,000.

WHERE THE TEAM IS TODAY— TACTICS AND STRATEGIES

Dortmund has great passing around the box. It's quick, and many players are involved. It feels like, "Now you see it, now you don't." It's tricky, thoughtful, crafty. It's accurate as well, and it comes from a wealth of skillful players. This is partly why Dortmund led the league last year. In doing so, it fielded a 4-2-3-1 or a 4-3-3 formation with phenomenal success. After all, if superior skill and individual player knowledge are considered in league with tactics and strategies, then Dortmund seems doubly blessed. Many coaches hope and pray for this. In fact, many teams find success based on player talent, and that alone. In the case of Dortmund versus the rest of the league: It really wasn't fair at times. Backing up Mario Götze were Marco Reus, Maximilian Philipp, Jadon Sancho, Thomas Delaney, and Christian Pulisic, along with other top-class performers. It was a club that kept pressing opponents, attack after attack.

Tactics and strategies: if it ain't broke, don't fix it; keep focused on the little things and implement outside defenders.

If you're the coach of Dortmund, you don't want to tamper with a good thing. Let the good times roll. Keep the formation in place, keep the lineup relatively unchanged, and allow the players to build on the momentum from last season.

Having said that, a good strategy to keep the players in proper spirits and committed to staying on top would be to stress the little things, which would be simple passes and simple connections. If the players get too wrapped up in grandiose plays and complicated schemes just because the team is operating a "high level," then it might just tear down the good things that have occurred so far. Sometimes the best players in the world reach a ceiling, and from that place they can say, "I'm continuing to get better," but in reality they can only stay as good as they are. At this ceiling, there's no getting better. Such examples would be

Messi, Pele, Michael Jordan, and Kobe Bryant. They can say things like, "I'm always improving. I'm always learning new things," but essentially, they're the standard. There's no getting better. They've achieved greatness.

So at this point, it's simple: Keep the greatness going. And when a player or team has reached the "highest point," then the best approach is to keep everything—that is to say, skills—fresh and roll forward in a positive direction. Appreciating a simple pass, both in making one and receiving one, is, oddly enough, a fine nuance of the game that will separate those who play well with world-class players. Borussia Dortmund has found this blissful "highest point," and to distinguish itself as the best team in the Bundesliga—and in Europe, for that matter—it needs to continue an appreciation of the simple things. Then its play should yield great results.

As Dortmund moves forward, keeping things simple, it should concentrate on implementing outside defenders into the attack even more. This would keep opponents off-balance and offer Dortmund new avenues to exploit in the attack.

LUCIEN FAVRE—A BRIEF COACHING PORTRAIT

Lucien Favre—born in 1957—is a former Swiss national team midfielder who played with Servette and Toulouse. He guided Borussia Dortmund from the sidelines last season with enormous success, and now the pressure is on for Favre to continue. On route to staying number one in the Bundesliga, expect to see a 4-2-3-1 or 4-3-3 formation. It brought the team success last year and will likely be repeated.

KEY PLAYERS AND
THEIR CHARACTERISTICS

Mario Götze, Marco Reus, Maximilian Philipp, Jadon Sancho, and Thomas Delaney

Mario Götze—the man who scored the World Cup winning goal for Germany in 2014—is a crafty goal-scorer with alert instincts around the box. He's not the quickest or the fastest, but he's quick enough and fast enough. His skill, touch, technique, and timing are few reasons he's knocked in over 25 goals during his two tours with Borussia Dortmund.

Marco Reus is a veteran and captain midfielder for Dortmund with an eye for goal. He's already played in over 150 games for his club with over 75 goals, an astounding feat.

Maximilian Philipp—born in 1994 in Germany—is an attacking player who was with SC Freiburg before landing in Dortmund. He played a significant role in Dortmund's 2018-19 season, and supporters are expecting more good things from him.

Jadon Sancho—born in 2000 in England—is a rising star with Dortmund and the English national team. Quickness, change of pace, elite skill, and a will to get by defenders are but a few attributes of this young talent. Keep on eye of Sancho for many great years to come.

Thomas Delaney adds a Danish presence in the midfield. The talented Dane brings experience from Werder Bremen, Copenhagen (where he played in over 240 games), and the Danish national team.

Overall Player Rating:
Mario Götze: 9
Marco Reus: 9.2
Maximilian Philipp: 8.8
Jadon Sancho: 9.3
Thomas Delaney: 8.7

KEY PLAYER STATS

(Total career goals with this club)

	Games Played	Goals
Mario Götze	137	29
Marco Reus	159	78
Maximilian Philipp	35	10
Jadon Sancho	42	12
Thomas Delaney	22	2

WHAT TO WATCH FOR ON TV—HOW MESSI, NEYMAR, RONALDO, AND OTHERS PLAY

Paco Alcacer—a forward with experience on Spain's national team—is part of a new wave of Dortumnd talent crashing on the scene. Should he stay with the team, he'll likely have a big impact. So far, Alcacer is a clearly one of the lead players. He's a goal-scoring machine. Watch for him on route to more scoring and excitement. Defenses will have a constant eye on him, that's for sure.

Christian Pulisic—an outside attacking midfielder and rising star with the USMNT—has done a little dance with Borussia

Dortmund, then Chelsea, and back to Borussia Dortmund on loan during the 2018-19 season. He should likely be back with Chelsea in June 2019. Though, as things stand, it wouldn't be unreasonable to see Pulisic back with Borussia Dortmund again. While he's not a fancy dribbler, he's an affective one who manages to sneak by defenders with speed and timing. Add to that his accurate passing, and you have a viable offensive threat every time around goal.

Axel Witsel—an experienced midfielder with over 100 games for Belgium—is an asset to have in Dortmund's lineup, and fans are expecting good things from him.

Lending a hand on defense in 2018-19 were Julian Weigl and Abdou Diallo; expect to see more from them.

Leading the charge on the attack in 2018-19 were Mario Götze, Marco Reus, Maximilian Philipp, Jadon Sancho, Thomas Delaney, and Christian Pulisic. Should this group say together throughout the 2019-20 season, then, without a doubt, more good things are around the corner for Dortmund.

WHAT ARE THEIR CHANCES OF WINNING THE LEAGUE TITLE THIS YEAR?

Very good.

Overall Team Ranking: 9.4

RB LEIPZIG

Twitter: @DieRotenBullen @RBLeipzig_EN
Founded in 2009
German Champions: 0
European Cup and UEFA Champions League: 0
UEFA Super Cup: 0

Known For
Very passionate fans
Exciting games
Controversy
Red Bull Arena
Ralf Rangnick
Yussuf Poulsen
Diego Demme
Willi Orban

A BRIEF TEAM HISTORY

Dietrich Mateschitz—an Austrian who co-founded Red Bull—
was a leader behind the efforts of Red Bull GmbH to form RB
Leipzig which came to fruition in 2009. Very quickly the team

moved up in the ranks from lower divisions in German soccer to the top Bundesliga.

RB Leipzig is a controversial club, to say the least. Since its inception, there have been protests lingering, following the team like an unwanted tax bill from the IRS. Rory Smith of *The New York Times* wrote: "At Hansa Rostock, supporters refused to enter the stadium for the first 10 minutes; at Union Berlin, fans dressed in black and remained silent for 15 minutes. Only last week, when RB Leipzig traveled to Dynamo Dresden for a German Cup match, a section of the home crowd threw a blood-soaked bull's head at the field."[11]

To an outsider this might seem odd. One might think: *It's a new team. What's the big deal? What's the fuss all about?* Rory Smith captured where some of the controversy originated from: "The problem is encapsulated in the RB Leipzig name. Officially, RB stands for RasenBallsport—a neologism meaning 'lawn ball'—but it takes only one glance at the team, its uniforms, its stadium or its $30 million training base to see through the disguise. To many, RB Leipzig will never be anything more than another marketing venture started by the Austrian energy-drink maker Red Bull."[12] Furthermore: "Unlike the English Premier League, though, where outside investors are welcomed and the game's authorities are officially 'ownership neutral,' Germany jealously protects what is known as its 50+1 model, in which clubs are regarded as social institutions that must be majority-owned by their members. Red Bull's arrival ran counter to all that."[13] Therein lies a lot of the reason for the animosity toward RB Leipzig.

Today, games are played in Red Bull Arena, which has a capacity of over 42,959. Originally, the stadium was called Zentralstadion, which started up for business back in 1956 (following construction which began in 1954).

Currently, something's going on with Leipzig. There's excitement in the air. Things are on a roll. It's a club in the middle of a good run, making history with each game.

FACTS ABOUT THEIR CITY

Leipzig is located in Saxony, a state in the central-eastern section of Germany, with a population of around one million people in the greater metropolitan area. A beer garden in Leipzig worth trying is Schrebers Restaurant und Biergarten. To date, Yussuf Poulsen of Denmark has the most caps for RB Leipzig with over 175 and counting.

WHERE THE TEAM IS TODAY— TACTICS AND STRATEGIES

Watch out for the 4-2-2-2, a formation used by coach Ralf Rangnick in the 2018-19 season.

Tactics and strategies: Leipzig needs to recruit widely and seize its potential.

As Leipzig continues to find its way through the top-level Bundesliga, it needs to acquire fresh talent in order to stay ahead of the curve. It has Red Bull money backing it along with advanced facilities; finding top players shouldn't be too overwhelming.

Leipzig is a team that, despite all the criticism, is ready to reach the very peak of its potential this season, which, in Leipzig's case, would potentionally be third place in the Bundesliga. How will it get there? And how might it possibly surpass third place and win the league? For starters, Leipzig has concentrated on its elite training facility. Rory Smith, writing for *The New York Times*, pointed out: "For all the controversy about the source of the team's wealth, it is hard to argue with how RB Leipzig has spent it. Its training base is ultramodern, with individual relaxation spaces for the players; a light, airy cafeteria; and an indoor, artificial-turf sprint track to gauge players' strength and speed."[14]

Additionally, coach Ralf Rangnick's approach is "attractive and expansive"[15] as the team presses its opponents, and things click.

This combined with training local youth players, strong recruitment, and a coach who can relate his philosophy to his players will make for a very interesting development.

RALF RANGNICK—A BRIEF COACHING PORTRAIT

Ralf Rangnick was born in 1958 in West Germany and played as a defensive midfielder and eventually transitioned to coaching. He's led a number of teams including TSG 1899 Hoffenheim, Schalke 04, and, most recently, RB Leipzig. As a player he never reached the big time, and as a coach he's right in the middle of it. For a club that's had such an upward bound start since 2009, Rangnick is guiding this Leipzig ship through tumultuous waters while finding a safe place to dock. And many more good results are expected this season.

KEY PLAYERS AND
THEIR CHARACTERISTICS

Timo Werner, Diego Demme, Willi Orban, and Tyler Adams

When the ball drops, **Timo Werner** is ready to go. Werner has been blasting away goals with speed, agility, and a fierce eye for simply getting the ball in the net. The German international forward is on a roll, and goals keep piling up. He'll go up against any Bundesliga forward and will likely come out on top. Quite simply, he'll make his team better.

Diego Demme—born in 1991 in Germany—has made a quick pit stop with the German national team; with Leipzig he's one of leaders on the team, guiding the offense from a defensive midfield position. Leipzig fans—rocking the house at Red Bull Arena—will be counting on Demme for his leadership and organizational ability.

Willi Orban, the captain and leader on defense, has the responsibility of guiding the club forward and into the Champions League. He previously played at 1. FC Kaiserslautern and represents Hungary's national team. He'll use these experiences to help navigate through the tumultuous waters of leadership.

It's safe to assume **Tyler Adams** is pretty familiar with Red Bull energy drink. He played youth soccer with New York Red Bulls, then he transitioned to the New York Red Bulls first team in Major League Soccer in the US, and now he's playing with RB Leipzig, which, of course, is owned by Red Bull. As an up-and-coming American midfielder with the US men's national soccer team, Adams is a good defender and promotes quick offensive tempo.

Overall Player Rating:
Timo Werner: 9.5
Diego Demme: 8.5
Willi Orban: 8.5
Tyler Adams: 7.7-8

KEY PLAYER STATS

(Total career goals with this club)

	Games Played	Goals
Timo Werner	90	48
Diego Demme	161	1
Willi Orban	108	11
Tyler Adams	9	0

WHAT TO WATCH FOR ON TV—HOW MESSI, NEYMAR, RONALDO, AND OTHERS PLAY

Despite the protests, and general disdain toward the club, Leipzig continues to move forward, finding success and proving it belongs in the Bundesliga. Some players that provided a useful presence in the 2018-19 season included Timo Werner, Diego Demme, Willi Orban, Ibrahima Konate, Marcel Halstenberg, and Lukas Klostermann.

Emil Forsberg—a Swedish international midfielder—has a lethal shot from around the top of the box which defenses should pay close attention to.

Yussuf Poulsen—who previously represented the Danish club Lyngby Boldklub—has played in over 175 games for RB Leipzig and has tallied up over 45 goals as well. Watch for the Danish international to continue his scoring ways as Leipzig makes a strong run this season.

While Leipzig is fighting off the protest atmosphere wherever it goes, proving that it belongs in the Bundesliga, the 2019-20 season will be an exciting, telling, challenging, and revealing one for a new club destined to make a name for itself.

WHAT ARE THEIR CHANCES OF WINNING THE LEAGUE TITLE THIS YEAR?

Anything is possible. It's a team that will be close to the top again, however, it will be difficult for Leipzig to surpass Bayern Munich and Borussia Dortmund.

Overall Team Ranking: 8.9-9.1

THE UNDERDOGS

TSG 1899 Hoffenheim
Schalke 04

TSG 1899 HOFFENHEIM

Twitter: @achtzehn99_en
Founded in 1899
German Champions: 0
European Cup and UEFA Champions League: 0
UEFA Super Cup: 0

A QUICK GLANCE

TSG 1899 Hoffenheim was founded in 1899, and it's a club building from last season with big ideas. In fact, based on the 2018-19 season, which was a very competitive one for the club, don't count Hoffenheim out. With a little retooling, it has a strong chance to move up in the rankings and do some damage throughout the league. On route to a great season, a few players that stand out are Nadiem Amiri, Ishak Belfodil, and Andrej Kramarić. Along with experience, they add depth and will lead the cause up front for Hoffenheim throughout the long season. There's a strong, dynamic group of support players in the lineup, and, without a doubt, Hoffenheim will be a team to contend with in 2019-20. Will it win the league outright? No, but watch for Hoffenheim as it's a team on the rise.

Overall Team Ranking: 8.3

SCHALKE 04

Twitter: @s04_en
Founded in 1904
German Champions: 7
European Cup and UEFA Champions League: 0
UEFA Super Cup: 0

A QUICK GLANCE

Schalke 04—which was founded in 1904—is no club to laugh at. It had a very good year in 2018-19, and a lot is expected coming into this season. Breel Embolo will be counted on for goals, while Guido Burgstaller, Daniel Caligiuri, and Suat Serdar will be adding a nuanced touch to the attack. True, things didn't end as well as they could have in 2018-19; the team was low in the standings; it didn't have a chance at winning the league, much less placing in the top three. But the 2019-20 season is a new one, and Schalke is a club that can certainly dash for the finish line in better form. Watch out for Schalke. Big things could be underway for it this season.

Overall Team Ranking: 7.1

SPAIN—PRIMERA
DIVISIÓN LA LIGA

A Look Back: 2018-19

Top Players: Lionel Messi, Luis Suarez, Philippe Coutinho, Gerard Pique, Jordi Alba, Arturo Vidal, Gareth Bale, Luka Modric, Marcelo, Karim Benzema, Toni Kroos, Antoine Griezmann, Koke, Saul Niguez, Ever Banega, Franco Vazquez, Pablo Sarabia, Roque Mesa, Jesus Navas, Daniel Parejo, Jose Luis Gaya, and Rodrigo.

MVP: Messi.

The Teams
Barcelona
Real Madrid
Sevilla FC
Atletico Madrid
Real Betis
Alavés
Espanyol
Real Sociedad
Celta Vigo
Getafe
Real Valladolid
Girona
Villarreal
Valencia
Levante
Athletic Bilbao
Eibar
Rayo Vallecano
Huesca
Leganes

These were the teams from 2018-19 season. Going into 2019-20, there will likely be a rumbling in the standings. When teams want to win, and when teams strive to win, anything can happen… that's the beauty of each new season.

Leading the campaign of 2019-20 will be Barcelona, Real Madrid, and Atletico Madrid.

Top 5 Teams
Barcelona
Real Madrid
Atletico Madrid
Sevilla FC
Valencia

BARCELONA

Twitter: @FCBarcelona
Founded in 1899
La Liga: 25
Copa del Rey: 30
Supercopa de Espana: 13
European Cup and UEFA Champions League: 5
UEFA Super Cup: 5

Known For
Camp Nou
Strong attendance
Very passionate fans
Possession soccer
Cesar Rodriguez Alvarez
Laszlo Kubala
Johan Cruyff
Pep Guardiola
Luis Enrique
Diego Maradona
Romario
Ronaldo
Rivaldo

Ronaldinho
Xavi
Andres Iniesta
Carles Puyol
Sergio Busquets
Gerard Pique
Dani Alves
David Villa
Javier Mascherano
Lionel Messi
Neymar
Luis Suarez[1]

A BRIEF TEAM HISTORY

FC Barcelona stands out as one of soccer's world leaders with an expansive history and collection of championships. As of 2019, Barcelona has captured the La Liga an astounding 25 times, along with 30 Copa del Rey titles, 13 triumphant finishes in the Supercopa de Espana, 5 European Cup and UEFA Champions League championships, and, finally, 5 UEFA Super Cups. It's staggering when one sits back and rationalizes how hard it is to win only one European Cup and UEFA Champions League title.

Talent has been the name of the game at Barcelona. Any and all soccer prodigies mysteriously find their way to Camp Nou. Messi famously signed a youth contract on a napkin. Johan Cruyff, Diego Maradona, Romario, Ronaldo, Rivaldo, Ronaldinho,

---

1 Luis Suarez of Uruguay, not to be confused with Luis Suarez of Spain who was born in 1935. The latter Suarez was also a well-known player who represented Barcelona and Spain's national team. He also coached Spain from 1988-1991.

Henry, Zlatan Ibrahimovic, and Neymar are a few of the top brass that have adorned the steps of Barcelona's revered grounds, and there are plenty of others.

The coaching, for the most part, has been second to none. A few of the well-known greats are of Rinus Michels, Johan Cruyff, Louis van Gaal, Frank Rijkaard, Pep Guardiola, and Luis Enrique.

FACTS ABOUT THEIR CITY

The city of Barcelona—which is located on the northwester coast of Spain, overlooking the Mediterranean Sea—has a population of around 1.6 million people, while the metro area has approximately 5.4 million. Only a short distance from southern France, it's a well-traveled tourist destination with many delectable food and drink choices. A few beer options from Barcelona include Moritz and Estrella Damm.

While its food, drinks, and all-around tourist allurehelp set Barcelona apart, it also attracts players from the tech industry. The 2019 Mobile World Congress—a large event for products related to the mobile industry—took place in Barcelona. Such events continue to produce a historical chapter for Barcelona as a city intertwined with modern culture, a hub for contemporary innovators to shape the future.

Barcelona also holds on to simple charms and traditions. William Kennedy, writing for *The Atlantic* magazine, interviewed Gabriel García Márquez—the author of *One Hundred Years of Solitude*—in Barcelona on the Day of the Book. Kennedy wrote in 1973, "It is the custom on the Day of the Book for the city's publishing houses and bookstores to sell books in temporary wooden stalls on the main streets. By tradition, you buy a rose for your lady and she buys you a book."[16]

Soccer, however, stands above practically anything else in Barcelona. All the roses, books, and mobile phones in the world won't change that. Camp Nou—which came onto the scene in 1957—is the illustrious, awe-inspiring, stadium that Barcelona entertains and torments its opponents in. It continues to hold up as a classic soccer holy ground, with room for a little over 99,000 people.

WHERE THE TEAM IS TODAY— TACTICS AND STRATEGIES

Tactics and strategies: The trusty 4-3-3 will be called on often throughout the season, allowing Barca to dominate opponents with crisp possession soccer on route to another stellar year. Defensively, the 4-3-3 allows Barca the opportunity to push the tempo on defense at practically all areas of the field. Arturo Vidal is key in this area as he artfully guides the team in the transition from defense to offense. The presence of Vidal solidifies an already strong unit, though Vidal—a world-class, two-way player in his own right—is a unique piece on the board that should ensure a consistent winning season. Does Barcelona need help with tactics and strategies? One would think not. Although, staying ahead of the curve is paramount for the club. As Vidal gets past his prime, the club will need to replace him with a strong player. Certainly, as with any club, these developments are happening behind the scenes. For now, as long as Vidal stays injury free, things should be good for Barca in the near future. But one thing is clear: Hang on to Vidal for as long as possible and get as much out of him as you possibly can.

The art of closing the deal is best displayed by Barcelona. Once it has a lead, a win is pretty sure to follow. This has practically everything to do with possession-minded soccer, often known as "tiki taka." The well defined and somewhat cruel tactic of keep-away soccer has been mastered by Barca; it can be safely assumed that any player who has worn the blue-and-red jersey has a PhD in keep-away. While some critics swear that Barcelona's overall possession-oriented approach—commonly known as "tike taka"—is "boring" and "negative" soccer, there are plenty of proponents that have realized it's a cruel but necessary tactic for dominance on the soccer field, and, if appreciated through the right lens, it's aesthetically pleasing.

ERNESTO VALVERDE—A BRIEF COACHING PORTRAIT

Ernesto Valverde—born in 1964 in Spain—is a former forward with experience playing for Espanyol, Barcelona, and a few other clubs. He also managed to get one cap with Spain's national tem in 1990. Now, at the helm of his former club, he's leading one of the most storied teams in world soccer—a responsibility not to be taken lightly. In doing so he's inherited a quality team, though one that is transitioning from a generation of players that encapsulated Spain's "Golden Generation," such as Xavi, Iniesta, and Pedro. Those players—who shared the Barcelona stage with current Barcelona stars, Messi, Gerard Pique, Sergio Busquets, and Jordi Alba—have slowly dwindled away, as today's Barcelona lineup is a mere glimmer of yesterdays glory days, though it's a team with immense talent (as usual). Coach Valverde's challenge is to keep the train going with a high standard of quality front and center. Many people feel that Pep Guardiola is Barcelona's best coach ever. Perhaps that is a debate for another time. Though, it goes without saying, Valverde must live up to the standard laid down by Guardiola. Can he match the results of Guardiola? Can he reach that high? Time will tell, but he's off to a good start.

KEY PLAYERS AND THEIR CHARACTERISTICS

Lionel Messi, Luis Suarez, Philippe Coutinho, Gerard Pique, Jordi Alba, and Arturo Vidal

Messi is regarded, by many, as the greatest player of all time, even though he hasn't won a World Cup. However, he's taken care of basically everything else with the Catalonian giants, Barca. Sports writers have catalogued practically every move he's made, comparing him—rightfully so—to greats like Pele, Maradona, and George Best. Describing Messi's special talents, Daniel Alarcón of *The New Yorker* wrote, "No one can dominate a game quite the way he does; no one has the same combination of technique, speed, artistry, and lethal scoring prowess."[17] For over 10 years Messi has flaunted his stuff, becoming the leading scorer in Barcelona's coveted history. The ball stays on his feet like it was meant to be there, and he can shake off would-be defenders with a simple swivel and twirl of the body, a quick turn (almost like a pirouette), accompanied by a change of direction, with remarkable timing and instinct. Many players have great technique and can dribble well, but what sets Messi apart—in the dribbling department, anyway—is the ability to find the right moment in a game to elude well-trained opposition who eventually look like subordinates from a fourth-tier league that need to be subbed out. His scoring ability has only strengthened by his dribbling, which, combined with smart one-two passing combinations, has opened up countless opportunities for him over the years. Though he might not carry the same explosive speed he once showcased, Messi is still a relentless threat on the field, one Barcelona will likely hold on to for a few more years. Will he be traded? This is unknown. So far, he's spent the entirety of his professional career with Barca and distinguished himself as the best of the best.

Prior to his arrival in Barca, **Suarez** had been known to bite a few opposition players here and there, but since his time with Catalonia, he's become a gentlemen and regular man about town. Something about Camp Nou has brought him down to earth. Suarez is a goal-scorer. The Uruguayan finisher has uncanny instincts to find the back of the net with a presence around the box that is tenacious, skillful, crafty, deceptive, and instinctual. The once testy personality has found a way to become one of the classiest forwards in the game today, and Barcelona has proven to be a comfortable fit.

With the quick feet of **Philippe Coutinho** in the lineup, Barca has the luxury of a little Brazilian flair in the frontline alongside the dynamic duo from Argentina (Messi) and Uruguay (Suarez). Coutinho—who hails from Rio de Janeiro, Brazil—brings a rifle shot from anywhere around the box that makes life miserable for goalies, to say the least. Hopefully for Coutinho, the 2019-20 season will be a great opportunity to hit his stride.

Gerard Pique has been providing veteran leadership from the backline for years. He adds stability, wisdom, tranquility, and a trustworthy pulse for possession soccer.

At outside defense, the experienced **Jordi Alba** will give you steadiness on top of steadiness. He's a reliable possession-oriented player that might knock in a goal every now again, but his strength resides in his ability to keep passing combinations active along with a strong work rate on defense. These valuable assets should help Barca continue its winning ways this season.

Arturo Vidal—the midfield maestro—has been the engine that powers Chile forward, with all its success, including two consecutive Copa America championships in 2015 and 2016, and he's a great addition for Barcelona. He adds possession soccer awareness, deft touch, tough tackles, a perspicacious eye for defensive anticipation, along with an all-around grasp of the game that cannot be taught.

Overall Player Rating:
Lionel Messi: 10
Luis Suarez: 9.9
Philippe Coutinho: 9-9.3
Gerard Pique: 9.6-9.9
Jordi Alba: 9.1
Arturo Vidal: 9.8

KEY PLAYER STATS

(Total career goals with this club)

	Games Played	Goals
Lionel Messi	449	416
Luis Suarez	162	131
Philippe Coutinho	50	13
Gerard Pique	308	27
Jordi Alba	194	8
Arturo Vidal	29	2

WHAT TO WATCH FOR ON TV—HOW MESSI, NEYMAR, RONALDO, AND OTHERS PLAY

As usual, Barcelona has a roster resplendent in international talent: Argentina, Uruguay, Chile, Brazil, Croatia, France, Portugal, and, of course Spain. They all represent the Barcelona way: systematic destruction of opponents with brilliant and fastidious short passing combinations.

The experienced and subtle midfield awareness of Sergio Busquets is nothing but valuable for Barcelona. Barcelona will be without Iniesta and Paulinho from recent campaigns. Arthur Melo, who arrived from Gremio, should be available for action, like a well-crafted sports car in the midfield waiting to show off.

Messi will be leading the charge. Whether Messi scores or comes ever so close, there's excitement in the air. Joseph Wilson, whose work was published with the *Los Angeles Times*, laid out a bit of the tantalizing play one might see from Barcelona's highest scoring Argentine: "Messi had already gone close to scoring what would have been a brilliant goal when he dribbled around three defenders, sending two of them to the turf, before his low shot was tipped wide by goalkeeper Yassine Bounou."[18]

Vidal—the ultra-talented midfielder from Chile—will be available to add punch in the midfield. The remarkable passing skill of Ivan Rakitic will be on full display, backing up Messi with sound structure in the midfield. The steady wing-play of Jordi Alba will be omnipresent for Barcelona to continue its winning ways.

As a whole, Barcelona is a lethal offensive force that sucks the life out of its opponents with relentless, thoughtful, technically sound, and highly organized passing. Every time it takes the field, it evokes an artistic and intellectual curiosity surrounding the game it has tamed in such a way that makes a 90-minute match look like perfected art in motion.

WHAT ARE THEIR CHANCES OF WINNING THE LEAGUE TITLE THIS YEAR?

Amazingly good. Count on Barcelona being in the lead with strong competition from Real Madrid and Atletico Madrid.

Overall Team Ranking: 9.8

REAL MADRID

Twitter: @realmadrid
Founded in 1902
La Liga: 33
Copa del Rey: 19
Supercopa de Espana: 10
European Cup and UEFA Champions League: 13
UEFA Super Cup: 4

Known For
Strong attendance
Very passionate fans
Exciting games
Santiago Bernabeu Stadium
Ferenc Puskas
Alfredo Di Stefano
Raul
Luis Figo
Ronaldo
Zinedine Zidane
Roberto Carlos
David Beckham
Sergio Ramos

Iker Casillas
Cristiano Ronaldo
Marcelo
Gareth Bale
Luka Modric
Karim Benzema
Toni Kroos

A BRIEF TEAM HISTORY

When FIFA named Real Madrid "FIFA Club of the Century" in 2000, it was a no-brainer. Essentially, Madrid got off to a so-so start. For instance, when the European Cup—later known as UEFA Champions League—started out in 1955, Real Madrid only won the first five titles in a row. No big deal. Five titles? Yeah, we got that. Then, as years progressed, Madrid remained atop world soccer, typically fielding the best talent, winning the top prize in European soccer intermittently, graciously allowing others to have a try at it, eventually taking in 13 titles by 2018. The next best on the list would be AC Milan—another all-time great club—which has amassed a mere seven titles by comparison. Even Barcelona, who seems to always be winning the Champions League, only has gathered five titles. So leave the prize to Real Madrid: 13.

It's a club that's reigned supreme back to the days of Raymond Kopa of France, Ferenc Puskas, the Hungarian wonder, and Alfredo Di Stefano, the brilliant Argentine attacker with an air of classic soccer player floating around his every step. By this time, *Annie Hall, E.T. the Extra-Terrestrial, Beverly Hills Cop, Ghostbusters,* and *Back to the Future* weren't even movies yet;

the Cold War was waging; Frank Sinatra was making albums; Kurt Vonnegut was getting under way; Johnny Carson hadn't yet finished his 29-year-run; men were smoking cigarettes around the stadium, wearing fedoras, reading newspapers, and listening to the radio.

Then came Ramon Grosso, Amancio Amaro, and eventually, a few generations down the road, Raul, Steve McManaman, Roberto Carlos, Luis Figo, Ronaldo, Zidane, Angel Di Maria, Luka Modric, and Cristiano Ronaldo.

As Luka Modric and Toni Kroos steer the ship today, they're leading a group of guys who weren't even alive during Madrid's original five European Cup runs. So much has changed. Technology has upped its game since the Di Stefano days, switching from a radio-driven market to a social media-driven one, with Facebook, Twitter, and Instagram—a few outlets that keep the marketing departments of clubs like Real Madrid busy. With a heavy social media following comes sponsors eager to reach an active market.

On top of that, you have jersey sales, which, by comparison with the 1950s and 60s is a different game altogether, and few players in history have driven such sales like Ronaldo, Zinedine Zidane, David Beckham, and Cristiano Ronaldo—all Real Madrid players at one point in their careers.

As for recent soccer history being made, the 20th century "FIFA Club of the Century" has continued its winning ways, big time. For Real Madrid—a proven Goliath of clubs—2018 was a monumental year. Mark Ogden, writing for *ESPN*, captured a portion of the club's glittering accomplishments: "Zinedine

Zidane and his players created history by defeating Liverpool in the Champions League final in Kiev, Ukraine; Zidane by joining Bob Paisley and Carlo Ancelotti in the club of three-time-winning managers; and his players by not only delivering a third successive European Cup, but also extending Real's record haul to 13."[19]

But three might have been the magic number, for a time anyway. As it turns out, Cristiano Ronaldo—arguably Real's most influential player in the history of the mega club—was setting his sails slightly eastward toward Italy. During 2018, it was announced that Ronaldo would be leaving Real Madrid for Juventus. What? Three titles in a row with a chance to make it four consecutive trophies, and he's out the door? A shocker to say the least. Many people didn't see it coming. Essentially Ronaldo felt like the club's president (Florentino Perez) didn't appreciate him as he once did. The end result was Real Madrid's most impactful player in a century was leaving.

The departure of Ronaldo is a reminder of the ephemeral nature of athletic careers. In place of Di Stefano, Raul, Zidane, Ronaldo, and Cristiano Ronaldo, someone new will emerge. However, for now, in Ronaldo's place, are worthy bellwethers, including Karim Benzema, Gareth Bale, Marcelo, World Cup champion Toni Kroos, and Luka Modric who just happened to have won the 2018 Ballon d'Or (finally interrupting the 10-year back-and-forth between Ronaldo and Messi). Things are in good hands right now. Perhaps Madrid lost a big gun, but as time has shown, it's a club that keeps finding a way to win.

Having said that, Madrid took an embarrassing loss to Ajax in the 2019 Champions League, thus ending the three-year streak. As a result, it wouldn't be surprising to see a fresh look in the lineup sometime very soon. In March 2019, Zidane was rehired as coach. Surely, his reinstatement will provoke interesting conversations regarding future player recruitment. Sure, Madrid has a stable of amazing talent, but from the point of view of ownership and management, this is elite talent with a high trade value. So expect to see very interesting trades—history-making deals—in Real Madrid's future for the next year or so.

FACTS ABOUT THEIR CITY

Madrid, the fabulous capital of Spain, with a population of around 6.6 million people in the metro area, is one of the most popular places in all of Europe to visit. Its beautiful views, amazing architecture, exquisite food, and historical significance make it a must-visit city on anyone's wish list. Charly Wilder of *The New York Times* described Madrid's charming allure: "One of the best of the recently opened crop of modern tapas bars, Celso y Manolo knows what to update and what to leave alone. This goes for the stylish interior, with its preserved 1950s-era bar and floor tiles, as well as the menu, featuring reworked classics like grilled organic Cantabrian veal ribs with chimichurri (10 euros) or the chuletón de tomate, a luscious layering of avocado, mango, papaya, olive oil and fresh herbs on a half heirloom tomato (10 euros)."[20]

Onward to one of Madrid's most spectacular pieces of architecture. The renowned Santiago Bernabeu Stadium—which hosted the 1982 World Cup final match between Italy and West Germany—can hold a little over 81,000 people. Outside of multiple renovations and improvements, it's a cherished relic of soccer stadiums, having first opened its doors back in

1947. Within its walls are the ghostlike, shimmering, magical footsteps from that of Ferenc Puskas and Alfredo Di Stefano, the exhuberant cheers that have evaporated into the atmosphere, along with a flurry of discarded cigarettes from days of yore that have since been swept away with time. For any soccer fan or non-soccer-tourist, it's a must-see venue as it catches history in motion with each and every game.

WHERE THE TEAM IS TODAY— TACTICS AND STRATEGIES

Expect to see a 4-3-3 from the dazzling Real Madrid.

Tactics and strategies: Continue the strong passing combinations, release Gareth Bale into open space, and create more shooting opportunities for Marcelo.

Without a doubt, Madrid is one of the highest regarded passing teams in soccer on the planet. It shouldn't be a problem to keep this trend going, particularly with Luka Modric—a true passing savant—leading the way.

A nice option would be to get Gareth Bale out into open space more often, similar to how Kaka circa 2007 would run at multiple defenders. Bale has the wheels to disrupt things for opponents and this should be explored throughout the 2019-20 season.

Would it hurt to get more shots on goal from Marcelo? It seems as though he's content with passing in areas around the box or crossing whereas he could shoot for goal. Should he take a few more shots, this would spice things up nicely for Madrid while also keeping defenses off-balance. When Marcelo opts to pass or cross the ball too often, he becomes predicatable. The defense can anticipate him. A few more shots from Marcelo might, in fact, result in outright goals or create rebound opportunities for the forwards. More shots from Marcelo would also keep defenses honest and respect his ability to strike the ball, which would create more passing opportunities down the road. This isn't a do or die situation for Madrid's success, though it's a subtle point to consider.

Following the loss to Ajax in the 2019 Champions League, and the reinstatement of Zidane as coach, a lot of big changes might be underway. What sort of changes? Fresher legs and renewed energy. As for going forward, Madrid will surely make big trades to produce a new look.

ZINEDINE ZIDANE—A BRIEF COACHING PORTRAIT

Over the past few years, a bit of musical chairs has taken place in the coaching department of Real Madrid. Santiago Solari—a former midfielder with Real Madrid in the 2000s—served his national team for a handful of games. He replaced Julen Lopetegui (who replaced Zinedine Zidane. Solari and Lopetegui were a similar siutaiton. Essentially, Solari had taken the grim task of replacing Zidane, another former Real Madrid player (and arguably its best of all time), who turned into one of its most accomplished coaches after storming the castle of the Champions League final, earning a three-peat in 2016, 2017, and 2018. While Solari inherited a true Lamborghini of a team, it was still a challenge to live up to the standards of Zidane. Following the big loss to Ajax in the 2019 Champions League, Solari was put on a short leash. To say he might have been replaced would be an epic understatement. And then, guess what? In March 2019, not long after the Ajax defeat, team officials said enough is enough, and Zidane—the great savior of Madrid—was rehired. For fans of Zidane—who likely can be found at Real Madrid's Twitter account, with around 10.2 million followers as of March 12, 2019—his return was great news. Back in the saddle, Zidane is eager to get Real Madrid back to where its faithful following thinks it should be: on top of the world.

KEY PLAYERS AND THEIR CHARACTERISTICS

Gareth Bale, Luka Modric, Marcelo, Karim Benzema, and Toni Kroos

Gareth Bale—the Welsh international—trucks downfield with a powerful stride like a horse on race day, one to be cautious of if you're in the uncomfortable position of defending him. He's probably best known for his breathtaking goal against Barcelona back in 2014 in which he received a pass at midfield, then on his first touch took what seemed like the longest dribble in the world, playing the ball way out into space as if only he knew what was going to happen, only shepherded out of bounds by his defender. Then, after coming back in bounds, he regained a path to the ball, took it all the way into the box, and tapped it past the keeper for a goal. The Spanish announcers went wild. Though it wasn't necessarily on par with Maradona's unbelievable half-field run in 1986, it certainly conjured up a similar feeling. It was pure speed, power, and determination, a goal that set Bale apart as a dynamic playmaker.

Will Bale remain a part of Madrid? This is the 54-million-dollar question. Following a big defeat in the 2019 Champions League campaign to Ajax, there was talk of Bale moving on. Don't be surprised to see just that. At any moment, a player of his caliber can be sent elsewhere.

Luka Modric, the 2018 Ballon d'Or winner, is a passing phenom who will have all of his highly regarded midfield ability on display this season with skill, technique, touch, and field awareness. He is a player who acts with intuition in any situation. Following his second-place finish for Croatia at the 2018 World Cup, he has more experience to help guide Madrid closer to yet another Champions League title.

Marcelo has a little Brazilian pizazz combined with a steady European presence on outside defense. He'll keep the passing structure in place for Madrid; although, despite his quickness and tenacity, some may question his all-around defensive ability, a factor that could come into play this campaign.

Karim Benzema is now 10 years into his Real Madrid residency. The French striker is a true veteran with over 300 games for Madrid under his belt, along with more than 135 goals and counting. He's still got the finishing touch, coupled with acute technical ability, which makes him a force to be reckoned with in La Liga. On top of that, he's only in his mid-thirties, and ostensibly there are many more years for Benzema still left.

Toni Kroos has the unique perspective of being a 2014 World Cup champion and a 2018 World Cup flop. He knows firsthand how a team with enormous talent can go from first to worst in a mysterious heartbeat. His lessons learned from Germany can and should be applied to Real Madrid.

Overall Player Rating:
Gareth Bale: 9.8
Luka Modric: 9.9
Marcelo: 9.2
Karim Benzema: 9.1
Toni Kroos: 9.2

KEY PLAYER STATS

(Total career goals with this club)

	Games Played	Goals
Gareth Bale	154	78
Luka Modric	197	12
Marcelo	339	25
Karim Benzema	310	148
Toni Kroos	149	11

WHAT TO WATCH FOR ON TV—HOW MESSI, NEYMAR, RONALDO, AND OTHERS PLAY

Fluid, beautiful, attacking soccer would best describe Real Madrid, even without Ronaldo. He was the obvious driving force, but things will go on without him. Standout players from 2018-19 include Gareth Bale, Luka Modric, Marcelo, and Toni Kroos. Casemiro, the experienced Brazilian international, brought an organizational touch to the midfield, guiding the ball from Modric to Kroos, connecting everyone. In net was Thibaut Courtois, the highly regarded Belgian goalkeeper.

Isco is always a brilliant passing threat in midfield. Marco Asensio—another Spanish midfielder who's been on loan in the past—should be available for service. Vinicius Junior—who played for Flamengo at 16—is a talented Brazilian to keep an eye on.

As per usual, Madrid will be displaying all-star and World Cup-level soccer. Is it a team that can be stopped? With Ronaldo's absence, it definitely slowed down a bit last season. But slowing down a little bit for Real Madrid is a dream come true for the majority of clubs around the world. It's a team that lives by the highest standards possible, and with every season there comes an expectation to win, and win big.

But, having said that and after the resounding defeat Real Madrid took from Ajax during the 2019 Champions League campaign (which ended Madrid's streak), big changes could be underway. With Zidane back in charge of the team, a new look on the field might give La Liga an energetic spark very soon.

WHAT ARE THEIR CHANCES OF WINNING THE LEAGUE TITLE THIS YEAR?

Extremely high.

Overall Team Ranking: 9.7

ATLETICO MADRID

Twitter: @Atleti
Founded in 1903
La Liga: 10
Copa del Rey: 10
Supercopa de Espana: 2
European Cup and UEFA Champions League: 0
UEFA Super Cup: 3

Known For
Strong attendance
Very passionate fans
Exciting games
Wanda Metropolitano
Antoine Griezmann
Koke
Saul Niguez
Diego Costa

A BRIEF TEAM HISTORY

Atletico Madrid has earned second place in the European Cup (later renamed UEFA Champions League) in 1973-74, 2013-14, and 2015-16. On the plus side, it's won the UEFA Super Cup on three occasions. Within domestic competition, through the years, Atletico Madrid—known for its red, white, and blue colors—has done very well, winning La Liga 10 times, the Copa del Rey 10 times, along with two titles from the Supercopa de Espana.

FACTS ABOUT THEIR CITY

For years, Madrid, the illustrious capital of Spain, has been an active place for social and political issues. Around the globe, the introduction of Uber has competed with the taxi driving community for business, and the affects have filtered into the streets, including in Madrid. Recently taxi drivers have protested Uber, and, as Raphael Minder reported in *The New York Times*, "At Madrid's airport on Wednesday morning, some visitors were unpleasantly surprised to find the taxi stand filled with locked, empty vehicles, while striking drivers and airport workers instructed them to go back inside the terminal and join the lines at its subway ticket machines."[21] However people wind up getting to the games, Atletico Madrid president, Enrique Cerezo, welcomes fans—likely from one of the suites—in the Wanda Metropolitano stadium which holds 67,703.

WHERE THE TEAM IS TODAY—TACTICS AND STRATEGIES

The *Tao Te Ching* says in chapter 30 "For every force there is a counterforce,"[22] which would explain the role of Atletico Madrid to that of Real Madrid. The leader has always been Real while Atletico has been that counterforce—that other team in town trying to outdo its superior rival. Though it's had success over the years, Atletico always seems to be catching up. Despite recent strong showings, this remains true as Atletico—along with the rest of the world—watched on in awe as Real won three consecutive Champions League titles in 2016, 2017, and 2018. Though, if anything, Atletico—which has not yet won a Champions League title—could use its crosstown rival as inspiration. With a strong lineup featuring Antoine Griezmann, Koke, Saul Niguez, and Diego Costa, Atletico has been atop La Liga; in fact, at times, outperforming Real Madrid.

Tactics and strategies: utilize the 4-4-2 to its utmost potential and continue thriving with Griezmann as a creative force up top.

DIEGO SIMEONE—A BRIEF COACHING PORTRAIT

Diego Simeone—the former defensive midfielder, who, of course, spent many years on the Argentinean national team while also representing Atletico Madrid (among other clubs)—has fashioned this squad as a defensive force, reflecting his approach as a player combined with a twist of artistic ingenuity that has been best exemplified by his lead player Antoine Griezmann. Simeone, confident and passionate, has a few goals within his grasp, and those would be to dominate La Liga and win the Champions League. As usual, Atletico is so close. Simeone is hoping to push his side over that barrier into elite territory and this season should serve as a platform to achieve a legendary place within the hierarchy of Spanish clubs.

KEY PLAYERS AND THEIR CHARACTERISTICS

Antoine Griezmann, Koke, Saul Niguez, and Diego Costa

Antoine Griezmann—a crafty, skillful, and resilient attacking player who was rejected early in life in France for being too small, an experience which galvanized him to venture toward Spain—is at the forefront of Atletico's success and will continue to lead the charge during this 2019-20 season with a nuanced French touch.

Koke—born in 1992 in Spain—is a midfielder who has turned into a veteran with the Spanish national team with over 40 caps to date. He initially started out with Atletico Madrid B, and since then has attained over 270 appearances with the first team and still counting.

Saul Niguez—born in 1994 in Spain—started out with Atletico Madrid B and transitioned to the first team. He also has a number of games under his belt with the Spanish national team. As a midfielder, he's part of the pulse that brings out the best in Atletico Madrid.

Diego Costa was born in Brazil and has played a small amount of games with the Brazilian national team. He has since transitioned to playing for Spain's national team. He's played with a number of club teams, most recently with Chelsea and Atletico Madrid. Despite receiving a lot of criticism as a forward, particularly for his boring play, he's been a presence wherever he's gone. With Chelsea he scored over 50 goals. Now he's back with Atletico, looking to recapture some glory in La Liga.

Overall Player Rating:
Antoine Griezmann: 9.7
Koke: 9.3
Saul Niguez: 8.8-9
Diego Costa: 7.8

KEY PLAYER STATS

(Total career goals with this club)

	Games Played	Goals
Antoine Griezmann	175	94
Koke	275	30
Saul Niguez	153	18
Diego Costa	123	47

WHAT TO WATCH FOR ON TV—HOW MESSI, NEYMAR, RONALDO, AND OTHERS PLAY

Diego Godin of Uruguay, the team leader, will have help from Lucas Hernandez, Antoine Griezmann, Diego Costa, Jose Maria Gimenez, and others as Atletico Madrid attempts to finish first in La Liga with a strong push for the Champions League. While it's a team that's been chasing Real Madrid and Barcelona over the years, it has also distinguished itself as a firm competitor wherever it goes. Though overcoming Real Madrid and Barcelona for Spanish supremacy might be a difficult task, for Atletico, it's a passionate objective, one the team feels is within its reach.

Operating within a 4-4-2, Atletico has the tools, with its star player Griezmann leading the offense. With dynamic midfield support from Koke, Thomas, Hernandez, and Saul, Atletico is ready to flurry opponents with offensive pressure. This usually results in quick passing that doesn't rely on blind crosses into the box. As one of Spain's top teams, Atletico combines smart passing and tough defense to bewilder opponents.

WHAT ARE THEIR CHANCES OF WINNING THE LEAGUE TITLE THIS YEAR?

Good, but the leaders will likely be Barcelona and Real Madrid.

Overall Team Ranking: 9.6

SEVILLA FC

Twitter: @SevillaFC
Founded in 1890
La Liga: 1
Copa del Rey: 5
Supercopa de Espana: 1
European Cup and UEFA Champions League: 0
UEFA Super Cup: 1

Known For
Strong attendance
Very passionate fans
Exciting games
Jesus Navas
Dani Alves
Ever Banega

A BRIEF TEAM HISTORY

Sevilla's founding dates way back to 1890, around the time Jack Benny was born, which you know was a long time ago. Though it's a club without the grand allure of its neighbors—Real Madrid and Barcelona—it has remained relevant for some time. It's been a tough battle for Sevilla, after all, to constantly compete with two of the best clubs in world soccer. Though it's managed to get by—acquiring trophies intermittently, doing what it can.

Sevilla won the La Liga back in 1945-46. A long time ago, yes, but it's a competitive team nonetheless. It has captured five Copa del Rey titles and one Supercopa de Espana (in 2007 when Sevilla—which featured the speedy wing play of Jesus Navas—defeated the mighty giants, Real Madrid).

FACTS ABOUT THEIR CITY

Seville, which rests in the southern section of beautiful Spain, has a curious history. According to legend, Hercules founded the city of Seville.[23] Sure, why not? Today, it has a population of around 700,000 in the city and roughly 1.5 million in the metro area.

When it comes to dance and music, Seville—a short drive from Morocco—has a tradition of producing some of the best. A piece from *The New Yorker* illustrated a portion of the flamenco experience one would likely encounter in southern Spain: "Flamenco music and dance have existed since the eighteenth century, and today it's a tradition around the globe. But flamenco's roots remain strongest in its birthplace, Andalusia, a region of southern Spain, where it's performed in bars, dance halls, and on the streets. The music's classic forms, called *palos*, range from light-hearted and fun to mournful and passionate."[24] Essentially, if there's a moody dancer in southern Spain, Seville gets it.

Amid the rich culture of dance and music in the streets and bars, soccer stands above anything else as a cultural phenomenon. The coveted holy ground for Sevilla FC home games would be in Ramon Sanchez Pizjuan Stadium which dates back to 1958. Some 43,883 fans can pile inside to watch their local team work magic on the field.

WHERE THE TEAM IS TODAY— TACTICS AND STRATEGIES

The overall structure of the team is leaning toward greatness by way of a 4-4-1-1, a 3-4-1-2, or a 3-1-4-2. The latter is not the most highly recommended formation to push forward. Why? Using three defenders is always iffy, bordering on outright lunacy. The one defender in front of the three would indicate that it's a four-man backline, which, in essence it is. In essence, it would appear that Sevilla is comfortable with the 4-4-2. It's not the most affective formation in terms of pressing on defense, as it does not afford the team using it access to all parts of the field (as a 4-3-3 does).

Tactics and strategies: keep the ball going to Banega and improve in the forward department.

Despite the shortcomings of the 4-4-2, Sevilla was leaning on the productive midfield services of Ever Banega, Franco Vazquez, Pablo Sarabia, Ibrahim Amadou, Roque Mesa, Jesus Navas, and Quincy Promes during the 2018-19 season. Should Banega— the clever and skillful Argentine midfielder—remain with the team and if he can distribute the ball comfortably, good things should happen in midfield. Banega is a key asset to have moving forward—his success will produce good things for the rest of the lineup.

Sergio Escudero was vital for leadership and will continue to be counted on. Andre Silva, a Portuguese forward, was on loan from AC Milan; it will be interesting to see how he works out in the months to come. Without his presence, Sevilla is in desperate need of a world-class striker.

PABLO MACHIN—A BRIEF COACHING PORTRAIT

Pablo Machin—originally from Spain—has his hands full with a promising team, yet a group that is idling away in the middle of the pack. He may rely on his experience as a coach of Numancia and Girona for inspiration. While most people expect Sevilla to remain in the middle of the standings, Machin certainly has other things in store. The only problem is that Barcelona, Real Madrid, and Atletico Madrid will be standing in the way, as usual.

KEY PLAYERS AND THEIR CHARACTERISTICS

Ever Banega, Franco Vazquez, Pablo Sarabia, and Jesus Navas

Ever Banega is a classic, pure central midfield maestro with a gift for touch, passing, and crafty skill. He'll be sure to dazzle usual fans and fanatics alike with his gifts around the ball.

The brilliant **Franco Vazquez** was born in 1989 in Argentina and brings a little South American artistry to the field. His connection with Banega will be key for Sevilla's success.

Pablo Sarabia brings prior experience from Getafe and Real Madrid's reserve side. The attacking midfielder has over 90 games with Sevilla and a lot is expected of him this season from fans and owners alike.

Jesus Navas—who was born in 1985 in Spain—started his pro career with Sevilla, then shifted to Manchester City for a few years, and now has returned to where he began. As leader of the team, he relies on his experience from La Liga, the Premier League, and time spent with Spain's national team where he lit up the field with dynamic wing play. He's moving into his mid-thirties but still has some fuel in the tank to make a difference. He's one of those players who has a knack for getting behind defenders, a classic winger that always seems to be getting one step closer to the goal.

Overall Player Rating:
Ever Banega: 9.7
Franco Vazquez: 8.8
Pablo Sarabia: 8.4
Jesus Navas: 9.3

KEY PLAYER STATS

(Total career goals with this club)

	Games Played	Goals
Ever Banega	115	14
Franco Vazquez	83	13
Pablo Sarabia	94	23
Jesus Navas	333	25

WHAT TO WATCH FOR ON TV—HOW MESSI, NEYMAR, RONALDO, AND OTHERS PLAY

Generally speaking, whatever you're doing, whether it's building a house or completing an algebra problem, there exists a right way. There also exists a great passer, an organizer, a visionary, a crafty central midfielder, and that man would be Ever Banega, who showed off his capability on the grandest of stages when he connected with Messi for arguably the best goal of the 2018 FIFA World Cup. Banega sent a perfect chip right onto Messi's thigh, a perfect pass which enabled a perfect trap, which was controlled in stride and sent home for a goal—a perfect one–two punch. He is a true passing weapon on the field, but he needs help building things up; he can't do it alone. Nor can Jesus Navas, who, by comparison, is not someone that connects everyone with brilliant passes. He's been known to make quite a few nice setups, although he's more of a pass recipient who exploits the wing with relentless speed. However, the previous speed he displayed a few years ago is waning with age. In part, this is why Sevilla found itself knocking on the door of greatness but wasn't let in. With a few additions to the squad, just a couple tweaks here and there, things may fall into place. And a little bit more of a push is just what Sevilla needs to be on par with Barcelona. This isn't to say Sevilla is lacking talent. This is the conundrum of a team like Sevilla. After all, many of its players sprinkled La Liga with brilliance last season, including the likes of Franco Vazquez, Pablo Sarabia, Roque Mesa, and defender Joris Gnagnon. It's a quality side, no doubt. It proved this by lingering within the top of the standings in 2018-19.

Though something is holding Sevilla back. On its quest for greatness, it's struggling, as most teams do, with staying consistent and ahead of the curve. As Stephen Hawking wrote, "…disorder or entropy always increases with time."[25] This is something soccer teams try to avoid, clearly. Leading teams tend to have superior talent and coaches that can keep the talent functioning in orderly fashion. Indeed, number one teams stay one step ahead of the rest and keep squads like Sevilla slightly in catch-up mode. Can Sevilla reach number one? Can it keep things in order? Can it push Barcelona, Atletico Madrid, and Real Madrid back in the standings? Can it recruit new talent similar to how the Golden State Warriors landed the illustrious "advance to go card and collect $200" with Stephen Curry and Klay Thompson? These were two players no one thought would be as impactful as they ended up being, and their arrival subsequently catapulted a sub-par team to number one. In terms of player recruitment—which in effect is predicting the future—basketball and soccer are in the same boat. The issue Sevilla has is that it's hard to distinguish which players can positively change a club's future for the next 10 years. Even more so, it's hard, if not impossible, to determine which players will catapult a club to legendary status. Such recruitment is hit or miss.

With that said, a few strategic addendums to the lineup will do Sevilla some good. With the right touch it might end up dancing its way to the Copa del Rey, right past Barcelona, Atletico Madrid, and Real Madrid. At this point, it'll be a tricky dance, one that requires many lessons, a lot of experience, and all the right steps. And without a doubt, Sevilla needs a few special players to add an extra punch up front and redefine the overall program for a generation. Who those players will be, however, is an extremely intriguing development in southern Spain.

WHAT ARE THEIR CHANCES OF WINNING THE LEAGUE TITLE THIS YEAR?

Frankly, not too great.

Overall Team Ranking: 8.7

VALENCIA

Twitter: @valenciacf
Founded in 1919
La Liga: 6
Copa del Rey: 7
Supercopa de Espana: 1
European Cup and UEFA Champions League: 0
UEFA Super Cup: 2

Known For
Edmundo Suarez
Waldo Machado
Mario Kempes
Fernando Gomez Colomer
David Villa
Daniel Parejo

A BRIEF TEAM HISTORY

Valencia was founded in 1919, and over the years it has periodically achieved greatness. In the early 1940s, it began doing well domestically. A lot of this has gone under the rug a bit as Valencia is not widely regarded in the same class as Real Madrid, Barcelona, Bayern Munich, or Manchester United. Though, Valencia has accomplished quite a bit over the years, grabbing six La Liga titles, and on seven occasions it basked in the sun after winning the Copa del Rey.

Outside of Spain, Valencia won the UEFA Super Cup in 1980 (at the time it was called the European Super Cup.) Then, in 2004, it won the UEFA Super Cup again.

FACTS ABOUT THEIR CITY

Valencia—which adds a touch of Mediterranean culture to the east coast of Spain—has been known for its struggling economy (at least recently), good food, beautiful views, and the pulse driving the city which would be its soccer team, known in some circles as Valencia CF. The team plays in Mestalla Stadium, which dates back to 1923, and it holds around 49,800. Visiting for a game? Travelers might want to lodge at Vincci Lys. You can catch a train nearby while the hotel also has accessibility to local dining experiences.

WHERE THE TEAM IS TODAY—TACTICS AND STRATEGIES

Watch out for Valencia using the trusty 4-4-2.

A few members from the 2018-19 roster featured Ruben Sobrino, Rodrigo, Santi Mina, Kevin Gameiro, Daniel Parejo, Goncalo Guedes, Ferran Torres, Denis Cheryshev (who was on loan), Geoffrey Kondogbia, Francis Coquelin, Carlos Soler, along with defenders Jose Luis Gaya, Ezequiel Garay, Facundo Roncaglia, Mouctar Diakhaby, Daniel Wass (a versatile Danish talent), Gabriel Paulista, Cristiano Piccini, and Neto in goal. The 4-4-2 is a safe and straightforward approach to the game. One drawback is that it does not allow the players to evenly press on defense, unless midfielders are repositioned. For this group to do well, they might want to consider a new formation. Results to this point have proven to be middle of the road. Perhaps a 4-3-3 would spark a positive change as it would allow the team overall to press with more vigor on defense.

Tactics and strategies: The captains must step up and guide the team forward to higher ground.

Daniel Parejo, Jose Luis Gaya, and Rodrigo have been charged with leading the team, and the fans are starting to feel unsettled with average results. What can be done? That's for the captains and coaching staff to address before a mutiny ensues.

MARCELINO GARCIA TORAL—
A BRIEF COACHING PORTRAIT

Marcelino Garcia Toral—born in 1965 in Spain—has experience playing on Spain's youth national teams. He eventually played with Levante. After transitioning to the sideline, he's acquired coaching experience from Sevilla and Villarreal, among others, and now he's landed with Valencia. During the 2018-19 season, Valencia was coasting around seventh place. With a little effort from Marcelino, Valencia could be competing for what its fans would hope to be fourth place. The realistic chances of Marcelino taking down Barcelona, Atletico Madrid, and Real Madrid for La Liga supremacy are slim. He'll need to shake things up in order to achieve such a goal. This will require working with team management to isolate better opportunities in terms of offensive talent, along with a few defensive readjustments. As for this 2019-20 season, it wouldn't be surprising to see Valencia in sixth or seventh place. Nor would it be surprising to see Marcelino with a new club in 2020-21.

KEY PLAYERS AND
THEIR CHARACTERISTICS

Daniel Parejo, Jose Luis Gaya, and Rodrigo

Daniel Parejo, the captain, was born in 1989 in Spain and has a little experience with the Spanish national team. With Valencia, though, he has played over 230 games and counting. Outside of Valencia, Parejo, an experienced midfielder, has also spent time with Real Madrid, Queens Park Rangers, and Getafe. As a result, he's a suitable recipient of the captain's band, a position he holds going into the 2019-20 season.

Jose Luis Gaya—who is about 5'7"—was born in 1995 in Spain and has become a leader on the team. So far, he's been a Valencia player through and through. An outside defender, Gaya will be charged with shutting down the attack from opposition. In doing so, he has the weight of a fan base and management group to keep scores down and push his team forward in the win column. It's a big task, and one he's looking to deliver on.

Rodrigo was born in 1991 in the flamboyant Rio de Janeiro, Brazil. Usually found on the outside, he's an attacking player Valencia is depending on for goals. So far, he's done pretty well with Valencia, knocking in over 30 goals and has his sights set on more. The pressure is on to continue to play successfully and the 2019-20 season will be a strong opportunity for him to prove that he belongs with the team.

Overall Player Rating:
Daniel Parejo: 8.9-9
Jose Luis Gaya: 8.4
Rodrigo: 8.6

KEY PLAYER STATS

(Total career goals with this club)

	Games Played	Goals
Daneil Parejo	240	44
Jose Luis Gaya	145	3
Rodrigo	140	31

WHAT TO WATCH FOR ON TV—HOW MESSI, NEYMAR, RONALDO, AND OTHERS PLAY

Daniel Parejo, Jose Luis Gaya, and Rodrigo are leading the attack with Soler (number 8) adding a pulse at outside mid. Another threat on the outside in the form of Goncalo Guedes, a Portuguese international. Also adding support are Geoffrey Kondogbia, Cristiano Piccini, and Daniel Wass. Valencia is looking to interlace skill and team organization with a fluid pace to the game on route to achieving a much better La Liga result than last year's campaign. The fans are expecting this, management is idling away on making improvements, and the only thing holding Valencia back would be itself…and Barcelona, Atletico Madrid, along with Real Madrid.

This is the challenge Valencia signed up for; it's a great opportunity to show Spain, and the world, that it's ready to get out in front. With that comes the question of whether Valencia has the aptitude of being the world's next super-team. Can Valencia do it? This is tricky ground, and, to be honest, Valencia is not ready for it. A key aspect of being a super-team is to consistently stay on top, and the reality of this is that Valencia is not ready for such a thing. The lineup is just not at that level. Yet. It could happen, but not in the immediate future. Count on fourth place at best, or likely a seventh-place finish.

WHAT ARE THEIR CHANCES OF WINNING THE LEAGUE TITLE THIS YEAR?

Not exactly great. In fact, the answer is, no, Valencia will not win the league title.

Overall Team Ranking: 8.6

THE UNDERDOGS

Villarreal
Espanyol

VILLARREAL

Twitter: @VillarrealCF
Founded in 1923
La Liga: 0
Copa del Rey: 0
Supercopa de Espana: 0
European Cup and UEFA Champions League: 0
UEFA Super Cup: 0

Known For
Very passionate fans
Exciting games
Carlos Bacca
Gerard Moreno
Ramiro Funes Mori

A BRIEF TEAM HISTORY

Villarreal—which was founded back in 1923—placed second in La Liga in 2007-08. Aside from that, don't ask. Though it hasn't conquered Spain or Europe, it's a club with potential. And it's been seeking the optimal reach of that potential for the better part of 90 years.

FACTS ABOUT THEIR CITY

Villarreal (also spelled Vila-real) rests on the eastern seaboard of Spain, with a population of about 51,000 people. It's not the biggest city in Europe, or Spain for that matter, but it has great pride in its soccer team.

Sometimes cities and teams become associated with controversy outside the lines. Villarreal became known for a racist incident back in 2014 when a fan threw a banana at Dani Alves during a live game. As *CNN* reported, "Brazilian international Alves was taking a corner during Barca's 3-2 win when the banana landed at his feet. Maintaining his composure, Alves picked up the banana, peeled it and took a bite and got on with the game."[26] As a result, the club took action: "Villarreal issued a statement Monday saying it 'deeply regrets' the incident. 'The club has identified the person responsible and has decided to withdraw his membership card and prohibit access to the El Madrigal Stadium for life,' it added."[27]

The action taken by the club was a strong move in the right direction. Racist acts and words have become regular occurrences in many stadiums throughout Europe. The best way to combat such a thing is to act quickly and eliminate such behavior. After all, outside of the Dani Alves incident, Villarreal has a charming atmosphere it would prefer to showcase at its Estadio de la Ceramica stadium, an intimate venue that holds around 24,890 people.

WHERE THE TEAM IS TODAY— TACTICS AND STRATEGIES

Expect to see a 3-5-2 formation. Carlos Bacca, Gerard Moreno, Karl Toko-Ekambi, Santiago Caseres, Pablo Fornals, Vicente Iborra, Mario Gaspar Perez, Bruno Soriano, Jaume Costa, Victor Ruiz, and Ramiro Funes Mori were called upon in the 2018-19 campaign that fell short of a championship.

Tactics and strategies: Possibly the formation needs to be re-evaluated, specifically the use of three defenders. It's not the best approach, according to many schools of thought. The idea is that four defenders provide a better, more reliable, foundation for a team to move forward. Of course, it could be right to point out that a central midfielder can double as a central defender. But, hold on, it's still three defenders, right? Needless to say, coach Javier Calleja is an experienced soccer mind—some may say brilliant. Though, sometimes, an idea or a passion for something overwhelms common sense. Sometimes reality gets shrouded by a grand vision. Perhaps, when it's all said and done, purveyors of a three-man defensive line are correct after all. In the meantime, four defenders would probably be more advantageous for the club. Results may or may not get better, but such a move will definitely be one to watch for as the season progresses.

JAVIER CALLEJA—A BRIEF COACHING PORTRAIT

Javier Calleja—whose full name is Javier Calleja Revilla—was born in 1978 in Spain. The former midfielder played with Villarreal, Alcala, and a few other teams before transitioning to coaching whereby he landed different positions within the lower ranks of Villarreal before assuming the lead role with its first team. Should he catapult Villarreal to the top five in Spain, it would be a huge undertaking. However, he certainly intends to try.

KEY PLAYERS AND THEIR CHARACTERISTICS

Carlos Bacca, Gerard Moreno, and Ramiro Funes Mori

Carlos Bacca is a dynamic and speedy forward from Colombia. After 50 games with his national team, Bacca is the kind of South American threat Villarreal is expecting to yield big results.

Gerard Moreno—a formidable forward from Spain—has plenty of past experience with Villarreal before he tested the waters with Mallorca and Espanyol. Now he's back with Villarreal, looking to make a big splash.

Ramiro Funes Mori is a relatively new addition to the club, one that brings experience from Everton and River Plate. The Argentinean defender also has a number of games under his belt playing for his national team. Hopefully, he and the defensive back unit can improve upon last season. The team's owners and fan base are counting on it.

Overall Player Rating:
Carlos Bacca: 8.7-8.9
Gerard Moreno: 8.2
Ramiro Funes Mori: 8.8

KEY PLAYER STATS

(Total career goals with this club)

	Games Played	Goals
Carlos Bacca	63	21
Gerard Moreno	65	14
Ramior Funes Mori	17	1

WHAT TO WATCH FOR ON TV—HOW MESSI, NEYMAR, RONALDO, AND OTHERS PLAY

Some of the talent featured last season includes the Colombian forward sensation Carlos Bacca, Gerard Moreno, Karl Toko-Ekambi, Santiago Caseres, Pablo Fornals, Vicente Iborra (who brought some experience from Leicester City to the table), the experienced Mario Gaspar Perez, Bruno Soriano, Jaume Costa, Victor Ruiz, and Ramiro Funes Mori.

Head coach Javier Calleja has been credited with recruiting well, but one may argue otherwise. After all, his team struggled in the standings throughout last season, so, on paper, one has to wonder if recruiting can be improved upon...or was it just one of those bad luck seasons?

Watch for a team lurking in the middle of the pack, a team with fascinating internal talent, a team with moments of brilliance, a team trying to find a consistent winning formula.

WHAT ARE THEIR CHANCES OF WINNING THE LEAGUE TITLE THIS YEAR?

This is a club that has had a decent to good presence in La Liga, though not an outright contender for the Champions League title. Its chances of becoming the best team in Spain this year are laughable at best, and terribly low at worst. Though, as an underdog team, it has everything to play for, and you never know, an athletic miracle could indeed happen.

Overall Team Ranking: 7.3

ESPANYOL

Twitter: @RCDEspanyol
Founded in 1900
La Liga: 0
Copa del Rey: 4
Supercopa de Espana: 0
European Cup and UEFA Champions League: 0
UEFA Super Cup: 0

A QUICK GLANCE

Espanyol—which was founded in 1900—had an average year in 2018-19, and it's hoping to improve drastically during the 2019-20 season. Certainly, no one is expecting the team to win the league outright. That would be a goal beyond its dreams. At this point, gaining a foothold in the top eight teams of La Liga would be more realistic. However, this might prove to be very challenging. In fact, it will be a very steep hill to climb. For Espanyol to get into the top five a lot has to be done. It needs to make a few key trades, improve its forward line, improve goal production, and get more consistency out of the lineup defensively. Fans of the club really need for Borja Iglesias, Esteban Granero, and Marc Roca to come up big. Even then, it will take somewhat of an athletic miracle for Espanyol to reach the top three in the standings. However, if it's going to get it done, then there's no better time to start than right now. Under the leadership of Víctor Sánchez and Javi López, two of its more experienced players, there is hope. There exists a right way, and it's up to Espanyol to find it.

Overall Team Ranking: 7.9

ITALY–SERIE A

A Look Back: 2018-19

Top Players: Cristiano Ronaldo, Douglas Costa, Mario Mandzukic, Paulo Dybala, Alessio Romagnoli, Hakan Calhanoglu, Krzysztof Piatek, Lucas Paqueta, Lautaro Martinez, Joao Mario, Samir Handanovic, Marcelo Brozovic, Ivan Perisic, Daniele De Rossi, Diego Perotti, Edin Džeko, José Callejón, Arkadiusz Milik, and Piotr Zieliński.

MVP: Cristiano Ronaldo.

The Teams
Juventus
Napoli
Fiorentina
Internazionale
Sassuolo
Genoa
Lazio
Sampdoria
AS Roma
Parma
AC Milan
Torino
SPAL
Udinese
Bologna
Atalanta
Cagliari
Empoli
Frosinone
Chievo Verona

These were the teams from 2018-19 season. Going into 2019-20, there will likely be a rumbling in the standings. When teams want to win, and when teams strive to win, anything can happen… that's the beauty of each new season.

Top 5 Teams
Juventus
AC Milan
Inter Milan
Roma
Napoli

JUVENTUS

Twitter: @juventusfcen
Founded in 1897
Serie A Titles: 35
Coppa Italia: 13
European Cup and UEFA Champions League: 2
UEFA Super Cup: 2

Known For
Strong attendance
Very passionate fans
Exciting games
Dominant teams
Elite talent
Dino Zoff
Michel Platini
Paolo Rossi
Zinedine Zidane
Andrea Pirlo
Cristiano Ronaldo

A BRIEF TEAM HISTORY

Since 1897, Juventus has entrenched itself as a classic Italian club, one revered around the world. It's made big moves, leaving in its wake a flurry of championships and a legacy of winning. Up until now, it's gathered over 30 Serie A titles. But, hold on. Recently, Juve has literally dominated Serie A. It has overwhelmed Serie A. It has soared high above Serie A like a hawk from the royal mews, peering down on the lowly competition as if it were mice waiting to be eaten for dinner. It won consecutive titles in 2011-12, 2012-13, 2013-14, 2014-15, 2015-16, 2016-17, 2017-18, and 2018-19. Simply put: Yikes. This is insanely good, bordering on "Boston Celtics in the Bill Russell era" good.

Is Juventus that good? Or has the competition dwindled away as more elite players have recently migrated to Spain, Germany, and England, as opposed to in the past when the world's best preferred the rich landscape of Italy? Indeed, Serie A is not what is used to be, but, make no mistake, it is still a premier league with players of the highest caliber. Perhaps this is a discussion for another time. For now, Juve definitely has Italy by a firm grip. One it has been relishing, for sure, because, after all, as they say in Italy (where soccer reigns supreme), goals are worth their weight in gold. Without a doubt, Juve's recent run of success is astounding. Soon, someday anyway, the grand team from Turin will likely acquire 36 titles and then move onto 54 and 72 and 108. When it comes to Italian clubs, it seems like there's no stopping Juventus.

Over the years, there has been some kind of gravitational force in northwest Italy. Juventus has attracted world-class talent including the likes of Michel Platini, Paolo Rossi, Zinedine

Zidane, and Andrea Pirlo. Prior to these players, Juve got on the board when its star Omar Sivori—a forward who wound up representing the national teams of Argentina and Italy—won the Ballon d'Or in 1961. Then came the illustrious era of Platini during the 1980s whereby Juve experienced a lot of success. By way of the Ballon d'Or, Juve players took center stage with Paolo Rossi winning it in 1982 (the same year he won the World Cup with Italy), and Platini—France's phenom before Zidane—grabbed the award in 1983, 1984, and 1985. Writing for *The New York Times*, Alex Yannis captured an aspect of Platini's charm back in 1984, during his prime with the renowned Italian club: "Knowledgeable fans immediately distinguish Platini, too—but for his remarkable skills, ingenuity, elegance and vision. He makes himself visible because he executes the unexpected to perfection."[28] Then, a few years later, Zidane—representing the black-and-white jersey of Juve—took home the Ballon d'Or in 1998; he was Platini's French successor, yet another colossal talent Juve managed to coral under its lucrative wing.

Most recently, in 2018, Juventus took the world by surprise after signing Cristiano Ronaldo, which, as it turns out, may have been the biggest acquisition in the club's illustrious history. This is the same Ronaldo who signed a huge billion-dollar deal with Nike in 2016. Writing for *CNN*, a report from Ahiza Garcia stated, "With his new Nike deal, Ronaldo becomes the third athlete to sign a 'lifetime' endorsement with the company."[29] In doing so, the Portuguese star reached rare air. "Nike also has 'lifetime' deals with NBA greats Michael Jordan and LeBron James. Details about Ronaldo's deal were not released, but the partnership will remain in effect even after he retires."[30] As *Forbes* reported, "The lifetime endorsement deal is reportedly similar to James' pact and worth as much as $1 billion."[31]

Outside of Ronaldo being a special once-in-a-lifetime player, why did Juventus sign a superstar nearing his mid-thirties? According to Rory Smith of *The New York Times*: "They did so, partly, because the 33-year-old Ronaldo represented the club's best chance of ending its long, agonizing wait to win a third Champions League title. Juventus has lost two of the last four finals, to Barcelona in 2015 and to Real Madrid, and Ronaldo, in 2017. Despite seven straight Serie A titles under his stewardship, to Andrea Agnelli, Juventus's president, going one step further in Europe now ranks as somewhere between a mission and an obsession."[32] It was a bold move. One that caught the world's attention, to say the least.

Evidently, Juventus sold 520,000 Ronaldo shirts on the initial day he was announced with the legendary Italian side. The Agnelli family—which also owns Fiat and Ferrari—knows how important Ronaldo will be for wins and sales. Just how far he'll guide the club forward is yet to be seen.

FACTS ABOUT THEIR CITY

Turin, located in northwest Italy, has a population of around 880,000 people.

Writing for *CNN*, Jeanne Bonner—who had been to Italy before—wrote, "...Indeed, one thing had not changed in my absence: Italians still seek face-to-face contact—even in the digital age. This is especially so in Turin, a city of large squares and historic cafés.

The site of the 2008 Winter Olympics, Turin is surrounded by mountains and criss-crossed by trams and cyclists. Being outdoors is second nature. Turin is covered in porticos, or covered walkways, where you can stroll no matter the weather."[33] Jeanne added, "Turin played a pivotal role in the Risorgimento, when Italy became an independent country. But this type of memory-laden travel is less about visiting historic places and more about exhausting a personal bucket list. So rather than visiting all of the 'can't miss' spots, I rented a bike and tooled around Turin like a native, stopping at an outdoor flea market where I proceeded to argue with merchants over prices."[34]

When it comes to supporting the local team, there's no debate. People of Turin love Juve and have been supporting the black-and-white stripes for generations. As for "the direction of the team"—that may strike up a lively debate.

WHERE THE TEAM IS TODAY— TACTICS AND STRATEGIES

Juventus has a great deal of leverage with the frontline of Cristiano Ronaldo, Douglas Costa, Mario Mandzukic, and Paulo Dybala. These are a few featured players, and good ones at that. While plenty of others contribute to the overall success of the club, one approach in particular might want to be used above all else.

Tactics and strategies: Give the ball to Ronaldo.

It's a pretty good strategy, one argued by millions of fans throughout thousands of bars around the world. Essentially, as simple as it may sound, it's a good strategy. The after effects of getting the optimum amount of touches to CR7 will benefit Costa, Dybala, and others. One drawback of getting too much of the ball to CR7 is that, when it's all said and done, chemistry throughout the team may suffer. (It could successfully be argued that Portugal has suffered from such an approach over the years; when everything goes through Ronaldo others end up standing about, becoming sluggish.) Essentially, his move from Real Madrid to northwest Italy precipitated—in a good way—an interesting conversation: How much of the ball should Ronaldo get? It's an intricate juggling act that coach Massimiliano Allegri must administer with great wisdom.

MASSIMILIANO ALLEGRI— A BRIEF COACHING PORTRAIT

Massimiliano Allegri was born in 1967 in Italy and eventually played midfield with a ton of teams, some of which include Napoli and Cagliari. As a coach, just prior to landing with Juventus, Allegri was in charge of AC Milan. Since 2014, he's done well with Juventus, and with the addition of Ronaldo things are looking even better. Watch for a 3-4-2-1 or a 3-4-1-2 or a 3-1-4-2 or even a 4-4-2…Essentially, Allegri favors slightly different looks, with a strong backline, dependable midfielders, with varying options of forward threats all working in sync.

KEY PLAYERS AND
THEIR CHARACTERISTICS

Cristiano Ronaldo, Douglas Costa, Mario Mandzukic, and Paulo Dybala

Cristiano Ronaldo—one of the most marketable players in the history of the game, who signed a lifetime billion-dollar deal with Nike in 2016—has a plethora of skills to keep his game going strong even into his mid-thirties. In the past, particularly during his time with Manchester United, his dribbling prowess on the wing stood out ostensibly more than anything else. Now, with time, he has showcased his aerial dominance to the fullest, along with his deadly free-kick ability that continues to keep goalkeepers up at night. A few questions remain: Will Ronaldo walk away with the Ballon d'Or yet again? Can Ronaldo lead Juventus to a Champions League title? In the next five years, should he avoid serious injuries, he will have every opportunity to conquer these challenges—with a defiant flexing of the muscles—and it wouldn't be surprising to see him reaching these goals at the tailend of his career.

Douglas Costa—a quick, fast, and tenacious Brazilian winger—is ready to tantalize defenses with his telling runs that often leave defenders a few steps behind if not completely in the dust. As a result, defenders, unluckily, end up superseding one another in a desperate attempt to keep Costa in his place—good luck. His change of pace is top level, and he uses this talent to get behind opponents—which might as well be cones—inevitably opening up opportunities in and around the box. Juventus management is counting in this for big results this season.

Mario Mandzukic—a Croatian forward who received a second-place medal at the 2018 World Cup—has an eye for goal, a usable option up top. While he doesn't have dazzling dribbling ability, his approach is more of "Lewandowski meets Luca Toni."

Paulo Dybala—a rising Argentine star—brings an eye for goal up top as one of Juventus' leading forwards. Lo and behold, with over 120 games played and over 55 goals scored, he's on the way to legendary status in northern Italy.

Overall Player Rating:
Cristiano Ronaldo: 10
Douglas Costa: 9.7
Mario Mandzukic: 7.9-8.1
Paulo Dybala: 9.3

KEY PLAYER STATS

(Total career goals with this club)

	Games Played	Goals
Cristiano Ronaldo	27	19
Douglas Costa	48	5
Mario Mandzukic	117	30
Paulo Dybala	125	57

WHAT TO WATCH FOR ON TV—HOW MESSI, NEYMAR, RONALDO, AND OTHERS PLAY

Juventus has been leading Italian soccer, and there's no reason to think the 2019-20 Serie A season will be any different. There's a sound structure to the team. It exudes Italian quality with a hint of international flair. Throughout the lineup, there's plenty of punch coming from Cristiano Ronaldo, Douglas Costa, Mario Mandzukic, and Paulo Dybala which is balanced out by the two strong men leading defense, who also have a vast amount of experience with Italy's national team: Giorgio Chiellini (the captain) and Leonardo Bonucci.

Juventus, the Italian leaders, the team with a dream to recapture the Champions League, is deadset on conquering Europe and increasing the durability of a renowned Italian brand, a legitimate leader in the history of soccer around Italy and the world. In February of 2019 a piece by James Masters of *CNN* read, "For so long, Juventus has dominated in Italy, winning seven successive league titles with an eighth almost inevitable."[35] Indeed Juventus finished first in Serie A in 2018-19. So many league titles in a row is an amazing feat. "But it is the Champions League crown that it craves. Ronaldo was supposed to be the man to deliver for a club that has lost out twice in the final in the past four years."[36]

Unfortunately, even with Ronaldo, Juventus didn't bring home the Champions League title in 2018-19. It lost to Ajax. Though it had a great Serie A season in 2018-19 and will likely continue this path in the 2019-20 campaign.

While excitement is in the air with every touch Ronaldo takes, Juve is an experienced club, one—it could be argued—that borders on outright brilliance, with multiple facets of offensive resplendence.

Though, it can't be ignored, with the acquisition of Ronaldo, Juventus is back in the center of prime time; with that move, Serie A is also front and center. Should Messi, Neymar, and Mbappé make a switch to Serie A, then it will be revving on all cylinders—similar to the 1980s and 90s.

For now, though, Juve is leading the cause, taking the spotlight, relishing in it, flourishing in it, flaunting its black-and-white jersey wherever it goes, making history with every touch of the ball. This is a magical time for Juventus and Italian soccer. It's turned into must-watch TV and Juve—featuring Ronaldo, Costa, Mandzukic, Dybala, Chiellini, and Bonucci—will not disappoint.

WHAT ARE THEIR CHANCES OF WINNING THE LEAGUE TITLE THIS YEAR?

Very, very high.

Overall Team Ranking: 9.7-9.9

AC MILAN

Twitter: @acmilan
Founded in 1899
Serie A Titles: 18
Coppa Italia: 5
European Cup and UEFA Champions League: 7
UEFA Super Cup: 5

Known For
Strong attendance
Very passionate fans
Exciting games
Franco Baresi
Ruud Gullit
Marco van Basten
Frank Rijkaard
Paolo Maldini
Roberto Donadoni
Demetrio Albertini
George Weah
Alessandro Costacurta
Alessandro Nesta
Andrea Pirlo

Andriy Shevchenko
Gennaro Gattuso
Kaka
Alexandre Pato
Ronaldinho
Alessio Romagnoli

A BRIEF TEAM HISTORY

AC Milan. The name alone conjures images of prestige, trophies, and dominance. As a club that's been around for over a century, it has flourished throughout multiple generations. Initially, AC Milan kicked things off with domestic titles in 1901, 1906, and 1907. In the 1950s and 60s, it earned multiple Serie A titles, while also capturing the European Cup in 1962-63 and 1968-69. Those years set the stage for the illustrious 80s and 90s; AC Milan conquered Europe in 1988-89, 1989-90, 1993-94; it eventually repeated as Europe's finest in 2002-03, and 2006-07. In terms of winning the UEFA Champions League (formerly known as the European Cup), AC Milan ranks second of all time. (In first place is Real Madrid with 13, followed by AC Milan with 7. Liverpool has 6. Bayern Munich and Barcelona have 5 titles each.)

In recent years, domestically speaking anyway, AC Milan won the Serie A in 2010-11, and since then it has been regrouping and keeping up with league leader, Juventus. On its way back to the top, there was a rumbling in 2017, and a coaching change was made. Soccer fans around the world heard the big news as media outlets jumped all over it. Tom Sunderland from the *Bleacher Report* wrote, "Vincenzo Montella has been relieved of his duties as AC Milan manager, with the club's former midfielder Gennaro

Gattuso immediately installed as his replacement."[37] Gattuso had been head coach of AC Milan's youth department. His appointment imbued new life into Milan. Though, in true Italian fashion, it hasn't been without some intrigue. There was talk of Arsene Wenger replacing him. Gattuso had assumed the role with pride. "But Wenger," as reported in 2018 by Rory Marsden, writing for the *Bleacher Report,* "with his immense experience and remarkable track record with Arsenal, is arguably a much safer pair of hands to guide Milan back into the European elite."[38] Whether or not Wenger—or indeed another coach—comes in to replace Gattuso, there's so much to look forward to in Milan.

FACTS ABOUT THEIR CITY

Milan has opened its doors to—yes—a Starbucks outlet. Now Italians, lovers of coffee who are used to the best, have an opportunity to try the renowned Starbucks, a company that, in part, was inspired by Italian coffee bars many moons ago. Indeed, it was an interesting move by Starbucks to attempt a cultural breakthrough in Milan. Writing for *CNN*, Silvia Marchetti reported, "The truth is, for all the fanfare surrounding the new 'Reserve Roastery,' including the long lines outside, it's unlikely to have much of a long-term impact on locals. Italians love their espresso on the run."[39] Perhaps that's true. On the other hand, it might be a trendsetter. On route to the San Siro, which holds a little over 80,000 people, fans might indeed stop by Starbucks.

Then again, fans might make a pit stop to sip some Italian beer such as Ghisa, Forst Premium, or perhaps Birra Moretti (which has been acquired by the Dutch giant, Heineken).

WHERE THE TEAM IS TODAY—
TACTICS AND STRATEGIES

The new coach for AC Milan will possibly continue with a 4-3-3. This is yet to be seen. A lot will be on the plate for the new coach and the decicion of a formation will be interesting moving forward. Last season, during 2018-19, solid contributions came from Hakan Calhanoglu, Krzysztof Piatek, Suso, Fabio Borini, Lucas Paqueta, Tiemoue Bakayoko, Lucas Biglia, Franck Kessie, Ricardo Rodriguez, Alessio Romagnoli, Mateo Musacchio, Davide Calabria, Andrea Conti, and Diego Laxalt. Yet it wasn't enough to push the club over the top and past league leader, Juventus. While the off-season allowed for a chance to regroup, Gattuso and company will be back with a vengeance, resembling—no doubt—the tough style of play its coach was widely known for.

With that said, AC Milan is a club leaning on youth and experience. The youth rests in the hands of Lucas Paqueta, an up-and-coming talent from Brazil, along with Alessio Romagnoli; a lot is expected of these two players, and the results should be very interesting in the next five years or so. A portion of AC Milan's experience is represented by Ignazio Abate. Abate—born in 1986—is a reliable and steady option at outside defender with over 235 games played with AC Milan. He's tallied up a little over 20 games serving the Italian national team, but that boat may have passed. For now, he's a firm fixture with Milan, leading the team with a great deal of experience from the back.

Tactics and strategies: Stay strong on defense and stay within the top four in Serie A.

Staying strong on defense may be easier than staying within the top four in Serie A, though it could be assumed that a strong defense will inevitably yield results worthy enough of remaining in the top four. And that's were AC Milan needs to be in order to surge forward by season's end with a strong push for the Serie A title. In addition, simply put, it needs to acquire superstar talent in order to seriously take over Italy's top league. This is a serious issue the club, its management, and coaching staff need to evaluate in the near future. As for what to watch for on TV, fans certainly have been anticipating—and hoping for—big moves from management. After all, Barcelona and Real Madrid, along with a few other salient European powerhouses, have been thriving in the past 10 to 15 years with the world's elite talent, something AC Milan was once highly known for. We'll touch on this issue again momentarily, but first let's take a look at AC Milan's coach.

MARCO GIAMPAOLO— A BRIEF COACHING PORTRAIT

Gennaro Gattuso—a former AC Milan standout midfielder and Italian World Cup 2006 champ—took over the position of coach for AC Milan in 2017 and since then he managed to guide the team in a positive direction, but not without rumours of being replaced by Arsene Wenger (the former longtime coach of Arsenal). It seemed that AC Milan wouldn't have a replacement for him, but they finally hired a new coach, Marco Giampaolo. He is looking to take the club to new heights. Having coached a number of teams, including Sampodoria and Empoli, he might just be a brief replacement coach. Still, with support from the fans, Giampaolo has an opportunity to reach number one in

Serie A. The challange is great, and with a new coach in place, AC Milan will be watched with interest for the next year or so.

KEY PLAYERS AND THEIR CHARACTERISTICS

Alessio Romagnoli, Hakan Calhanoglu, Krzysztof Piatek, and Lucas Paqueta

Alessio Romagnoli—AC Milan's captain—has acquired over 110 games thus far as a steady center back. He also has experience playing for Roma and Sampdoria, not to mention the Italian national team. Born in 1995, Romagnoli is an emerging leader within the Italian soccer structure. Expect to see much more of him in the years to come.

Hakan Calhanoglu—born in 1994 in Germany—is an attacking midfielder who, despite being born in Germany, plays for Turkey's national team where he's surpassed 40 caps. With AC Milan, he's been a force to reckon with since 2017.

Krzysztof Piatek—born in 1995—is a Polish forward who hopped from playing with Genoa to AC Milan in 2019 and is looking forward to making a strong impression during the 2019-20 season.

Lucas Paqueta is an interesting young Brazilian midfielder to keep an eye on. He has scant experience with Brazil's national team and recently joined AC Milan (after transitioning from Flamengo) to add some flavor in the midfield. He should be a strong asset for Milan moving forward.

Overall Player Rating
Alessio Romagnoli: 9.1
Hakan Calhanoglu: 8.4
Krzysztof Piatek: 8.1
Lucas Paqueta: 8.8-9

KEY PLAYER STATS

(Total career goals with this club)

	Games Played	Goals
Alessio Romagnoli	117	5
Hakan Calhanoglu	62	7
Krzysztof Piatek	13	8
Lucas Paqueta	11	1

WHAT TO WATCH FOR ON TV—HOW MESSI, NEYMAR, RONALDO, AND OTHERS PLAY

Drama always surrounds AC Milan. Sparks can fly when they meet crosstown rivals, Inter Milan. In 2019, emotions flared as the Rossoneri suffered a 3-2 loss. As *The Washington Post* reported: "Franck Kessie was visibly upset after being replaced by Andrea Conti in the 69th minute of Sunday's 3-2 derby loss to Inter Milan. The Ivory Coast international then grew even angrier and had to be held back by his teammates after Lucas Biglia said something to him."[40] Perhaps tensions within AC Milan's camp have more to do with the stress that builds up during a quest for first place than anything else. Such a quest—to reach the number one position in Serie A—is undoubtedly arduous. Without a doubt, AC Milan has a strong team; however, within the camp, some may be wondering out loud what many people are thinking when it comes to the actual roster. Because within the highly competitive landscape of Italian soccer, the Rossoneri are lacking one salient factor that should put the club over the top.

AC Milan needs to find superstar talent in order to dominate Serie A again. In fact, as things currently stand, AC Milan has a solid group. Perhaps though, it's a club searching for a true star, someone to push it over the top. As for now, a reliable, stable of talent has guided the team—along with it's enormous and demanding fan base—to good results, and some of those players from the 2018-19 season included Alessio Romagnoli, Ignazio Abate, Hakan Calhanoglu, Krzysztof Piatek, Suso (one of Milan's best attacking threats), Lucas Paqueta, Tiemoue Bakayoko (who was on loan), and Franck Kessie (who was also on loan).

Where are the supremely talented stars such as Ruud Gullit, Marco van Basten, George Weah, Andrea Pirlo, Andriy Shevchenko, Kaka, Alexandre Pato or Ronaldinho (albeit a Ronaldinho who had significantly slowed down)? Where are these types of players? Can AC Milan, for the sake of its fan base, legacy, reputation, and future, get ahold of Messi in the twilight of his career? Can it acquire Mbappé, Gareth Bale, or perhaps Neymar? It is, after all, AC Milan. No disrespect to the current pool of talent within the club, but, it's clear to see that Milan is struggling to find its way back to first place in Serie A. It's struggling to field true superstars, which is something past fans became accustomed to seeing. Can AC Milan find its glory days again? That magical formula? This remains to be seen, and it's a critical question for Leonardo Araujo—its sporting director—and a club that is second only to Real Madrid in all-time UEFA

Champions League titles. Leonardo, of course, played with AC Milan and was also part of Brazil's side during the 1994 World Cup. Also along for the ride is the sporting strategy and development director, Paolo Maldini—a veteran's veteran who gathered 26 trophies for the Rossoneri as a player. Both Leonardo and Maldini are great ambassadors for the game, with a vast amount of experience when it comes to winning on the field. With this wealth of knowledge, AC Milan is in a good position for success. But there's success and there's winning everything outright. AC Milan accepts nothing but the best, and a true effort to get back to the highest level is currently underway. A century from now, soccer historians will have time and hindsight to look back and study this current era, to evaluate what turn of events changed the course of history.As for its best efforts coming to fruition now, includeing signing star players and dominating Serie A again, fans will just have to wait and see.

WHAT ARE THEIR CHANCES OF WINNING THE LEAGUE TITLE THIS YEAR?

Good, but not great. It's a top five Serie A team building for greatness again.

Overall Team Ranking: 9.3

INTER MILAN

Twitter: @Inter
Founded in 1908
Serie A Titles: 18
Coppa Italia: 7
European Cup and UEFA Champions League: 3
UEFA Super Cup: 0

Known For
Strong attendance
Very passionate fans
Exciting games
Giuseppe Meazza
Giacinto Facchetti
Javier Zanetti
Ronaldo
Esteban Cambiasso
Julio Cesar
Zlatan Ibrahimovic

A BRIEF TEAM HISTORY

Inter Milan has won the Serie A 18 times: 1909-10, 1919-20, 1929-30, 1937-38, 1939-40, 1952-53, 1953-54, 1962-63, 1964-65, 1965-66, 1970-71, 1979-80, 1988-89, 2005-06, 2006-07, 2007-08, 2008-09, and 2009-10. Its last Serie A triumph was in 2009-10, a good 10 years ago. Under its belt are three UEFA Champions League (formerly known as the European Cup) titles from 1963-64, 1964-65, and 2009-10. As it turns out, 2009-10 was a great year for Inter Milan. Any time you can conquer Europe, it's a good year. In goal was Julio Cesar, with a strong lineup including brilliant outside defensive play from Javier Zanetti; central midfield guidance from Esteban Cambiasso; Cameroon's finest striker at the time, Samuel Eto'o; Argentinian striker, Diego Milito; and outside Brazilian defender, Maicon. The group was coached by Jose Mourinho, and its Champions League victory was the first return to glory since the 1964-65 conquest.

Since then, as far as Serie A is concerned, Inter Milan has stepped in line—with the rest of Italy's finest—behind league leader, Juventus. It's been a game of catch-up, and Inter is determined to be the first to dethrone the current champs.

FACTS ABOUT THEIR CITY

So many tourists from around the world flock to Milan for its food, wine, art, history, and culture. Clint Henderson, writing for *Fox News*, captured a hotel option for travelers: "One of the top hotels in Milan is the Excelsior Hotel Gallia. Maurizio Busani is the head concierge, and said the hotel is very special in that it 'marries contemporary aesthetics with the hotel's original Belle Époque style and remains over time one of Milan's historic landmarks.'"[41]

Travelers and locals alike would catch an Inter Milan game at the San Siro, which holds a little over 80,000. It's a well-known, historic stadium that's shared by Inter Milan and its crosstown rival, AC Milan. It got off and running in 1926 with multiple renovations since then. Outside of games played by Inter Milan and AC Milan it has hosted a score of international matches over the years. Notably, it was used during the World Cups of 1934 and 1990, and the latter became associated with the famous 1-0 defeat Argentina—the defending champs—suffered from the inexperienced Cameroonians, led by super-sub veteran, Roger Milla. As *ESPN* reported online, "In an amazing opening game, African football arrived on the world stage when Cameroon defeated the holders with a goal from Francois Omam-Biyik. Despite having two men sent off for some disgraceful tackling, Cameroon held on."[42] It was a spectacular game that kicked off the World Cup and shocked the world, writing a most interesting chapter in world soccer history.

WHERE THE TEAM IS TODAY— TACTICS AND STRATEGIES

Inter Milan could end up using a 4-2-3-1 or a 4-3-3 based its strategy from the 2018-19 season. It was a team featuring Lautaro Martinez, Mauro Icardi, Joao Mario, Ivan Perisic, Matteo Politano, Kwadwo Asamoah, Marcelo Brozovic, Roberto Gagliardini, Cedric, Stefan de Vrij, Andrea Ranocchia, Miranda, and Dalbert.

Tactics and strategies: Keep the team united and stay consistent to push Juventus out of first place.

Coach Luciano Spalletti was thrust into center court with some drama surrounding star striker, Mauro Icardi, as a result of Icardi's contract negotiations. Keeping the team unified and dedicated to the goal of winning Serie A will be of paramount importance for Spalletti—and his players—as the focus needs to be firmly set on dethroning Juventus from the top of Italian soccer. There's a great opportunity for Inter to surge forward and take the lead in Serie A, though off-field distractions are nothing but a hindrance in such a cause.

But one can't forget the two simple approaches that any team should abide by: Fast break first and fall back on possession second. One, fast break when it's available. That should be a team's first instinct. To catch the other team off-guard is good, and fast breaks should be the first option and used whenever it's possible. Secondly, if the fast break is not on, then revert to possession-oriented soccer. It's that simple. Or at least it should be. It's always that simple on paper, anyway. The question of how to use the wing talent is a salient issue and one that sometimes gets misconstrued.

With someone like Perisic out wide, it's tempting to just go right to him as often as possible. It would seem this is an "easy fix" and a "must-use" approach. The reality is such a thing wears out.

Also, to take it a step further (and this point can't be stressed enough), Inter should look to exploit the middle as much as possible; possession must be improved upon centrally and throughout the field. And then hit em' with the wings.

Sometimes, with talented wing players such as Perisic, a team has the propensity to go out wide for its attack. In doing so, it neglects the central positions. In fact, such an approach tends to look at the central positions as one-pass wonders that exist purely to get the ball out wide "where it belongs." Conversely, concentrating the attack on more possession play with central positions will inevitably open up *better* opportunities out wide for players such as Perisic.

This is not to say that Inter has intentionally neglected some of its central positions. Rather, should Inter be cognizant of such a thing and unify its efforts in this fashion, good things will come its way.

LUCIANO SPALLETTI—
A BRIEF COACHING PORTRAIT

Luciano Spalletti—who was born in 1959 in Italy—played as a midfielder for Empoli, along with a few other teams; Although, as a coach, he's reached a much higher plateau. Over the course of two decades, and some change, he's guided numerous competitive squads, including Sampdoria, Udinese, Roma, Zenit St. Petersburg, and Inter Milan. With the latter, Spalletti endured Mauro Icardi and his 2019 contract negotiations. *The Washington Post* reported, "Spalletti added that it was 'humiliating' for Inter's fans that it required negotiations with Icardi's lawyer 'just to get him to pull on the shirt that they love.'"[43] Spalletti, though, showed his resolve, and he moved forward with a team-first approach. Inter will need such guidance in the locker room if it has any plans of overtaking Juventus.

KEY PLAYERS AND
THEIR CHARACTERISTICS

Lautaro Martinez, Joao Mario, Samir Handanovic, Marcelo Brozovic, and Ivan Perisic

Lautaro Martinez—born in 1997 in Argentina—is a striker, and a young one at that, rising within Serie A and the Argentinian national team. He has a good shot around the box and plays with determination, a salient quality that should help him stand out in Serie A.

Joao Mario, a talented Portuguese midfielder, uses quick movement around the ball with connecting passes to keep the engine running. A big scorer? Nope. But he offers more on the organizational side of things.

Samir Handanovic, a 6'4" goalie with over 245 games with Inter Milan, is the team captain. He also brings over 80 games' worth of experience from Slovenia's national team. He's in his mid-30s and may not be the team's starting keeper much longer, but for now he still adds value in the net and with his leadership, which the club and fan base will count on for many shutouts.

Marcelo Brozovic—born in 1992—is a valuable Croatian midfielder to have on the field. His experience comes from more than 120 games played with Inter Milan as well as 40-plus caps with Croatia. His interactions with fellow countryman Ivan Perisic should prove fruitful for the Inter Milan faithful this season. It's usually beneficial to have such a combination on a club; the players are familiar with one another, and chemistry tends to be good.

Ivan Perisic—born in 1989—is a power player on the wing who lends Croatia a hand while he's not coursing through Serie A with Inter Milan. As most good attacking players go, he keeps defenders off-balance with constant threats down the wing, and as a result, he was a strong contributor last season and one of the reasons Inter Milan placed high. Inter Milan fans are lucky to have him on their side, and they'll be expecting more great results from the high-flying Croatian winger this season.

Overall Player Rating:
Lautaro Martinez: 8.8
Joao Mario: 8.8
Samir Handanovic: 9
Marcelo Brozovic: 8.6
Ivan Perisic: 9.2

KEY PLAYER STATS

(Total career goals with this club)

	Games Played	Goals
Lautaro Martinez	21	6
Joao Mario	61	4
Samir Handanovic	127	15
Marcelo Brozovi	127	15
Ivan Perisic	136	36

WHAT TO WATCH FOR ON TV—HOW MESSI, NEYMAR, RONALDO, AND OTHERS PLAY

Lautaro Martinez, Mauro Icardi, Marcelo Brozovic, Stefan de Vrij, Andrea Ranocchia, Miranda, Dalbert, and Ivan Perisic were a few players featured last season. With the confident goalkeeping of Samir Handanovic, it should be a group ready to make a move yet again this year. However, Inter Milan has much to strategize over.

Lazio will be chomping at the bit, looking to make a name for itself yet again. This should be of great concern for Inter as Lazio, Atalanta, Sampdoria, Torino, and Fiorentina were putting up a good fight in 2018-19. Don't forget Napoli, AC Milan, and Roma. But there's one thing nobody can forget. By the looks of it, that is to say, should things play out like in previous seasons, Juventus will be in the lead, and the rest of the pack will be in the hunt, competing to dethrobe the leaders from Turin.

Inter—featuring the attacking prowess of Lautaro Martinez and Ivan Perisic—should be in a strong position to make a push for the league title, though it will require a great deal of work, team chemistry, luck, and consistency.

WHAT ARE THEIR CHANCES OF WINNING THE LEAGUE TITLE THIS YEAR?

Good, that is to say, better than most Serie A teams, but Juventus is the leader. It will be challenging for Inter Milan to topple Juve, to say the least.

Overall Team Ranking: 9.4

ROMA

Twitter: @ASRomaEN
Founded in 1927
Serie A Titles: 3
Coppa Italia: 9
European Cup and UEFA Champions League: 0
UEFA Super Cup: 0

Known For
Strong attendance
Very passionate fans
Exciting games
Stadio Olimpico
Attilio Ferraris
Bruno Conti
Rudi Voller
Aldair
Cafu
Francesco Totti
Daniele De Rossi

A BRIEF TEAM HISTORY

While AC Milan, for instance, formed in 1899, Roma came around close to three decades later, in 1927, when three clubs[2] joined together to take on the big guns from the north—Juventus and AC Milan.

For a team that's won three Serie A titles and nine Coppa Italia trophies, Roma has fallen short of gathering the grand prize of the UEFA Champions League Cup. By far, throughout its history, Roma has been overshadowed by AC Milan and Juventus.

Talented players have circulated in and out of its locker room, such as Bruno Conti (a classic Italian winger), Rudi Voller (a prolific German scorer), Aldair (one of Brazil's great central defenders), and Cafu (easily one of Brazil's greatest outside defenders, if not the greatest).

In the modern era, Roma has been best known for Francesco Totti and Daniele De Rossi. Francesco Totti—who was born in Rome—played solely for Roma, amassing a little over 600 games as a midfield whizz. He has arguably been Roma's most renowned player over the years. Another Rome native, Daniele De Rossi, played by his side for years and eventually replaced Totti as captain upon his departure.

The last time Roma placed first in Serie A was back in 2000-01. Interestingly, to this day, it's still keeping up with the powerhouse clubs from the north: Juventus, AC Milan, and Inter Milan.

---

2   Foot Ball Club di Roma, Societa Sportiva Alba-Audace, and Fortitudo-Pro Roma Societa di Ginnastica e Scherma.

FACTS ABOUT THEIR CITY

Rome is an ancient city, dating back to the expansive Roman Empire and all its glory; a place that idolized gladiator sports in the Colosseum—think Russell Crowe in *Gladiator*. Other movies, such as the 1960 box office smash *Spartacus*—starring Kirk Douglas and directed by Stanley Kubrick—have depicted ancient Rome and its trials and tribulations…though perhaps not always accurately with regard to history.

It's one of those cities that has defined Europe and Western culture. Throughout each century, it's been a relevant force of nature, exuding a gravitational pull that draws excitement into it. In the modern era, or, to be specific, in the past hundred years or so, it still finds a way to define each generation.

It's a glitzy and bustling modern city, commingling with its overwhelming historic significance, and it has entertained many movers and shakers over the years, particularly in the film industry. Gore Vidal—an influential American writer who lived from 1925-2012—wrote a piece in *Vanity Fair* about his experience in the great Italian city:

"After the election of 1960, my friend Howard Austen and I moved to Rome not far from the classical library of the American Academy, where I daily worked on a novel about Julian the Apostate. Also during our first Roman years, in the Via Giulia and later in the Largo Argentina, movie production was at its peak, and, for a few years, many movies were made at Cinecittà, the principal Roman studio. During the late 50s I had worked on the script of *Ben-Hur* in an office next to that of the producer Sam Zimbalist. Farther down the corridor from my office, Federico

Fellini was preparing what would become *La Dolce Vita*. He was fascinated by our huge Hollywood production. Several times we had lunch together in the commissary. Soon he was calling me Gorino and I was calling him Fred. Neither Willy Wyler nor Sam wanted to meet him, because both were aware of a bad Italian habit which was to take over the expensive sets of a completed American film and then use them to make a new film. I think that this had happened with *Quo Vadis*."[44]

As far as taking over film sets, the same cannot be said about soccer clubs. Though some may argue the Stadio Olimpico—Roma's stadium which holds a little over 70,000 people—has been usurped by a few owners over the years.

Today, soccer continues to fill the headlines with a fierce obsession, garnering the sport much attention; so much, in fact, that it would rival any epic film, past, present, or future.

A few places to drop by for a beer around game time include BrewDog Bar, Open Baladin, and Roma Beer Company.

In-between drinks and soccer, perhaps visitors will find other outlets of entertainment.

From Bija Knowles and *CNN*, a few tips for travelers in Rome include: "The Trastevere area is great if you want to be near the thriving night scene, while hotels around Piazza Navona, Piazza del Popolo and Campo de' Fiori also provide short walks to good pizzerias, restaurants and bars from which you can also organize an efficient sightseeing plan of attack."[45] Like any big city, Rome has an added element of danger lurking around every corner. "The area around Termini has excellent hotels, but be warned that this is a less peaceful part of town, and you might not feel comfortable walking the streets around the station late at night."[46]

Perhaps some of these late-night celebrators will be members of an ultra group (very dedicated soccer fans; some of whom have resorted to violence from time to time).

Even still, this beautiful, historical city has so much to offer.

WHERE THE TEAM IS TODAY— TACTICS AND STRATEGIES

Judging from the 2018-19 season, Roma will likely rely on a 4-4-2 or 4-2-3-1. Some of the talent featured last season include Daniele De Rossi, Aleksandar Kolarov, Rick Karsdorp, Bryan Cristante, Diego Perotti, Edin Džeko, Aleksandar Kolarov, Lorenzo Pellegrini, Steven Nzonzi, Patrik Schick, Iván Marcano, Federico Fazio, Nicolò Zaniolo, Juan Jesus, Davide Santon, Kostas Manolas, Alessandro Florenzi, Javier Pastore, and Justin Kluivert.

Tactics and strategies: Strengthen the lineup for a push at the Serie A title. Unless Roma wants to continue floating around fifth or seventh place, it needs to recruit new, fresh, and different talent. It's nothing against the players currently in place, as they are definitely elite talent, but, clearly, in order to make positive strides in Serie A, a change needs to be made. The thing is, great players don't always equate to great team chemistry. What's lacking in Roma? A surge of talent to push the club over the top. Plain and simple. It's a good team without true star power. Get star power, and things will change for the better.

CLAUDIO RANIERI— A BRIEF COACHING PORTRAIT

Claudio Ranieri—born in 1951 in Rome, Italy—played defender with Roma back in his time. In the coaching ranks, he has led a vast number of teams, over 15, in fact, including Napoli, Juventus, Inter Milan, and the astoundingly explosive Leicester City during 2015-17. He landed with Roma in 2019, and the sky's the limit in terms of the optimism felt from the fan base. However, as coach, he can't do it alone; he certainly needs an influx of star power to create a big splash. Hopefully, for the sake of the fans and team management, Ranieri's arrival will push the squad forward to new heights, with Serie A and Champions League titles.

KEY PLAYERS AND THEIR CHARACTERISTICS

Daniele De Rossi, Diego Perotti, and Edin Džeko

Daniele De Rossi—who was born in 1983 in Rome—absolutely personifies Roma's jersey. He's a hometown kid and has only played professionally for Roma since 2001. The former World Cup champion from 2006 brings a vast amount of experience from his time with Italy and as a leader with Roma in Serie A. The Roma captain and midfielder, who patents his game off of Steven Gerrard, has acquired over 450 games played for his club and nothing seems to be holding him back at this point except for father time.

Diego Perotti—born in 1988 in Argentina—is a talented striker with experience not only with Roma in Serie A but also with Deportivo Morón, Sevilla, Boca Juniors, and Genoa, not to mention Argentina's national team whereby he's acquired five caps to date. He may possibly represent his home country again down the road, but for now the experienced forward is anticipating a great return to the lush fields of Italy with the Roma fans behind his every move. Thus far, with Roma, he's around the 20-goal mark and expectations in Rome for Perotti to put more points on the board are high.

Edin Džeko—born in 1986—represents the national team of Bosnia and Herzegovina when he's not playing with Roma. Playing for his country, he's knocked in 55 goals. With Roma, the 6'4" target player has tallied up 60 goals to date and counting. Perhaps though, he might be on his way out soon. He's pushing his mid-thirties and seeing that Roma needs a new feel in the lineup it might be close to the end for Džeko in a Roma uniform.

Overall Player Rating:
Daniele De Rossi: 9.3
Diego Perotti: 9
Edin Džeko: 7.8

KEY PLAYER STATS

(Total career goals with this club)

	Games Played	Goals
Daniele De Rossi	457	43
Diego Perotti	82	20
Edin Džeko	129	61

WHAT TO WATCH FOR ON TV—HOW MESSI, NEYMAR, RONALDO, AND OTHERS PLAY

Roma will come out of the tunnel looking for every opportunity to show that it's a contender for the Serie A title.

However, during the treacherous journey of conquering Italian soccer, Lazio will be one of many teams making things difficult for Roma. While it's watching out for Lazio, Torino, AC Milan, and Napoli, Roma, Romaneeds to maintain focus and keep its consistency up. Doing so will make things much easier for a team lacking true star power. True to form, De Rossi is a key player, but he's getting older, the club is relying on his steady play and leadership more than anything else at this time, and he's not in the class of Neymar or Messi or other similar talent. It cannot be ignored: Roma does not have this type of talent on the field. Still, De Rossi is a player who can successfully guide top-tier talent in the right direction with his solid contributions on the field, strengthened by his defensive prowess, along with his deep poo; of knowledge and experience, both on and off the field.

Yet, overall, Roma is searching for something that's currently slightly out of reach. Is Roma a good team? Sure. But something's not working. In order to reach the top of the league, someone has to make some bold moves and set this team in a different direction.

Watch for potential changes in the roster as Roma might come to its senses, make drastic trades, and make a strong case for itself to dominate Serie A.

WHAT ARE THEIR CHANCES OF WINNING THE LEAGUE TITLE THIS YEAR?

Not great, but there's hope.

Overall Team Ranking: 9

S.S.C. NAPOLI

Twitter: @en_sscnapoli
Founded in 1926
Serie A Titles: 2
Coppa Italia: 5
European Cup and UEFA Champions League: 0
UEFA Super Cup: 0

Known For
Strong attendance
Very passionate fans
Exciting games
Diego Maradona
Careca

A BRIEF TEAM HISTORY

Napoli was founded back in 1926 and has changed names a few times since. Overal, within its duration as a club, Napoli has two Serie A titles from 1986-87 and 1989-90. It also has five titles under its belt from the Coppa Italia (1961-62, 1975-76, 1986-87, 2011-12, and 2013-14).

The biggest move Napoli made came with the acquisition of Diego Maradona, who flourished in southern Italy from 1984-91, playing in 188 games and scoring 81 goals. For a few years, Maradona was joined up top by Brazilian great, Careca. Careca—a forward with with speed like a Ferrari who played with Napoli from 1987-93—thrived, and the two South Americans helped put Napoli in primetime.

During the 2018-19 Serie A season, Napoli placed well, and it intends on building toward a better tomorrow. That tomorrow does not include Maradona or any player near that level, but Napoli does indeed have a plethora of talent that has been surging forward in Serie A, with no intention of backing down any time soon.

FACTS ABOUT THEIR CITY

Naples—located in the southern portion of Italy on its west coast—has a population of around 966,000 people. Ranking above fine food and art would be the local soccer team, S.S.C. Napoli, which is overseen by Aurelio De Laurentiis, an experienced and well-known Italian filmmaker. He is one known for interesting opinions and lengthy, fascinating, talks. As Rory Smith from *The New York Times* wrote in 2019, "The trick, with Aurelio De Laurentiis, is to sit and to wait. He tends to take the scenic route through a conversation; his answers come wrapped in anecdotes and parables, laced with riddles and rhetorical questions."[47] Always ready to voice an opinion, Aurelio De Laurentiis represents Naples with no shortage of material for journalists. As Rory Smith wrote, "He is also never lacking an adversary, some villain standing in the way of progress, holding the game back through lack of imagination. His list has previously included not only UEFA but FIFA, Adidas, Nike, collective television deals and the Italian political establishment, among others. Many others."[48] He's definitely an owner with an opinion, interlaced with a touch of drama—something the people of Naples have been used to.

Napoli's games are played in Stadio San Paolo, which opened its doors back in 1959. Part of its renowned past has to do with one of the greatest players of all time, Diego Maradona—a walking soap opera. The Stadio San Paolo hosted the infamous 1990 FIFA World Cup semi-final between host nation Italy and Argentina (led by Maradona, who, at the time, was a member of Napoli), whereby Italy lost in penalty kicks. As a result of Maradona's attempts to quell the fans of Naples during this showdown—a game in which he actually asked for the local fans to support his Argentinian side—it may come as no surprise that about a year later, Maradona's time with Napoli (which had also been entangled with off-field antics) was up, and he found a new home with Sevilla. It's a stadium whose fans had both cheered Maradona on with the warmest embrace and conversely jeered at him with contempt. Today, this historic venue continues to host games for Napoli as one of Italy's premier athletic destinations.

WHERE THE TEAM IS TODAY— TACTICS AND STRATEGIES

As was the case in 2018-19, Napoli will likely go with a 4-2-3-1 or 4-4-2. A few players featured from last season include Dries Mertens, Fabián Ruiz, Simone Verdi, Amin Younes, Arkadiusz Milik, José Callejón, Lorenzo Insigne, Adam Ounas, Allan, Piotr

Zieliński, Mário Rui, Sebastiano Luperto, Kévin Malcuit, and Kalidou Koulibaly.

Tactics and strategies: In order for Napoli to continue its winning ways it needs to isolate possession as a key on its journey to reaching number one in the league. This is not to say that Napoli has no idea of what possession soccer is. Far from it. Though, as a team that is so close to number one in Italy, it needs to reaffirm its commitment to possession, take it very seriously, and thus improve its chances to stay consistent as the season moves along. This following point is a very important one to be made, and, one that should be repeated as much as possible: strong possession leads to consistency. This is key. Generally speaking (across the board and around the world), any club that neglects possession or dismisses it as something that is easily understood by pro level players is a club that is going to fail in the long run. Should Napoli really focus on improving subtle nuances in its possession game, then a true run at the Seria A title could be more of a reality than just a dream—a dream that has been just out of reach lately.

After all, Napoli is a good team. Would people be surprised if it won Serie A this season? Probably. Just because Juventus was so clearly out in front. But Napoli was right there, stride for stride with Juventus. Fans would have been much more surprised if SPAL, Udinese, Empoli, Bologna, Frosinone, or Chievo had ended up number one in the 2018-19 season; these clubs had potential (and certainly have potential down the road) to rise up and take down Juventus, but the chances of that were low, and, in fact, these clubs were ranked much lower than Napoli last season. On the other hand, Napoli was in the mix. It was a club to be reckoned with...a team that could've beaten the continent's best on any given day and needed just a little something extra to be number one. With some extra attention to detail, surely to be laid out by coach Carlo Ancelotti, it might just flip the world of Italian soccer upside down.

CARLO ANCELOTTI—
A BRIEF COACHING PORTRAIT

Napoli went with a true Italian legend for the job. This is the same Carlo Ancelotti that coached Juventus, AC Milan, Chelsea, Paris Saint-Germain, Real Madrid, and Bayern Munich. If there's a top-tier team, he's coached it. Prior to coaching he was a midfielder with Parma, Roma, and AC Milan, not to mention the Italian national team. He's a bit of a journeyman coach, but, given the quality of teams he has overseen, it's a journey well worth the effort. Now that he's settled in Napoli, he has a true challenge on his hands. Unlike the other pit stops, Napoli is not quite what he's been used to. The overall talent level with a commonplace Napoli roster will likely be a notch or two below that of Bayern Munich, Chelsea, and Real Madrid. Should he pull off a small miracle and thrust Napoli into the Champions League final, then, without a doubt, Napoli's fans will be ecstatic beyond belief. Is Ancelotti the man to do it? Can he pull it off? There's enough of a track record in his favor to suggest that if someone's going to make it happen, it might as well be him.

KEY PLAYERS AND THEIR CHARACTERISTICS

José Callejón, Arkadiusz Milik, and Piotr Zieliński

José Callejón—born in 1987 in Spain—is vice captain and a durable outside threat in the midfield. He also has experience playing with Real Madrid and Spain's national team to help bolster his leadership abilities with the team. While at Napoli, he's proven to be a long-term asset, having played in over 210 games to date with an impressive 60 goals.

Arkadiusz Milik—who was born in 1994 in Poland—is planning on bringing his A-game this season as a viable forward and scoring threat. In over 55 games played and 25 goals scored with Napoli to date, he's proven to be a strong presence up top. Some may argue that he's no more than a poor man's Lewandowski, yet Napoli is counting on great things from Milik.

Piotr Zieliński is part of a Polish connection with Milik, which fans and management alike are hoping will bring home big results this coming season. The midfielder has 100 games under his belt with Napoli so far, and he also has previous experience with Empoli and Udinese, thus establishing himself firmly in the arena of Serie A soccer and all the expectations that go along with it.

Overall Player Rating:
José Callejón: 8.6
Arkadiusz Milik: 8.3
Piotr Zieliński: 8.1

KEY PLAYER STATS

(Total career goals with this club)

	Games Played	Goals
José Callejón	216	60
Arkadiusz Milik	61	27
Piotr Zieliński	100	14

WHAT TO WATCH FOR ON TV—HOW MESSI, NEYMAR, RONALDO, AND OTHERS PLAY

First, you can't discount the contributions from Allan, Dries Mertens, Amin Younes, Lorenzo Insigne, and Kalidou Koulibaly. Then, on top of that, you have José Callejón, Arkadiusz Milik, Piotr Zieliński, thus making Napoli a very strong threat in Serie A, a true contender. It still has many hurdles in its way, namely Juventus, AC Milan, Inter Milan, and Roma. Lazio is close behind as well, and the list goes on. With Carlo Ancelotti as coach, this team might just be next in line to represent Italy as Serie A champions.

WHAT ARE THEIR CHANCES OF WINNING THE LEAGUE TITLE THIS YEAR?

Quite good, but not without a lot of things going its way.

Overall Team Ranking: 9.2

THE UNDERDOGS

Two Teams of Interest:
Fiorentina
Sampdoria

FIORENTINA

Twitter: @acffiorentina
Founded in 1926
Serie A Titles: 2
Coppa Italia: 6
European Cup and UEFA Champions League: 0
UEFA Super Cup: 0

A QUICK GLANCE

Fiorentina, led by coach Vincenzo Montella, is counting on plenty of goals from Giovanni Simeone. Meanwhile, its team leader, Federico Chiesa, has the responsibility of guiding the squad forward in a positive direction. This is a task that can be very tricky in Serie A. Along for the ride should be Jordan Veretout, Germán Pezzella, and Federico Ceccherini, to name a few. Out of 20 teams in the 2018-19 season, Fiorentina was right around the 10th position in the standings. It's a middle-of-the-pack team with a lot of room for improvement. The 2019-20 season will be a difficult challenge for the club, and the possibility of getting into the top five is highly unlikely. There will be a lot of competition from Napoli, AC Milan, Inter Milan, Parma, Torino, Lazio, and

Atalanta. Perhaps Fiorentina is meant to be in 10th place for next the few years. Perhaps it won't have enough manpower to push its way into the top of the standings. Certainly, there's no question that it's going to be difficult to advance past the top five teams. Without a doubt, its fans desire a league championship and are looking for better results than last season. The pressure is on. It should go without saying, Fiorentina needs to make big changes soon in order to grab ahold of elite status in Serie A.

Overall Team Ranking: 8

SAMPDORIA

Twitter: @sampdoria_en
Founded in 1946
Serie A Titles: 1
Coppa Italia: 4
European Cup and UEFA Champions League: 0
UEFA Super Cup: 0

A QUICK GLANCE

Sampdoria, a club that won the Serie A title back in 1990-91, has a great deal of work in order to get back to that place. Under its current coach, Marco Giampaolo, Sampdoria is looking for a big year in 2019-20. After all, with the arrival of Ronaldo in Juventus, Serie A is back with more excitement than it's had in a long time. Sampdoria now has a chance to show the world that it belongs on the same stage as the world's best clubs. Sampdoria's fans are ready for a tremendous showing and plenty of scoring. A few players from last season leading the charge this time around include Gastón Ramírez, an experienced player with the Uruguayan national team who has an opportunity to get more goals; Albin Ekdal, a midfielder from Sweden; and the captain

215

from 2018-19, Fabio Quagliarella. Quagliarella is getting up there in soccer years, and it's uncertain how long he'll continue at this level. However, if he can hang on for a year or two, his leadership will be vital for Sampdoria to make a push forward. It's certainly a crowded field of teams in Serie A, though, with a little concentration, a lot of goal production, along with some luck here and there, Sampdoria could find its way to a high place in the standings and thus create a more consistent standard of winning that could carry over for the next five to eight years.

Overall Team Ranking: 8.1

FRANCE–LIGUE 1

A Look Back: 2018-19

Top Players: Neymar, Mbappé, Angel Di Maria, Thiago Mendes, Jonathan Bamba, Loïc Rémy, Nicolas Pépé, Nabil Fekir, Moussa Dembélé, Memphis Depay, Wahbi Khazri, Yann M'Vila, Arnaud Nordin, Dimitri Payet, Morgan Sanson, Florian Thauvin, and Maxime Lopez.

MVP: Mbappé.

The Teams
Paris Saint-Germain
Lille
Montpellier
Saint-Etienne
Lyon
Marseille
Toulouse
Strasbourg
Bordeaux
Nice
Caen
Angers
Dijon FCO
Nimes
Stade de Reims
Stade Rennes
SC Amiens
AS Monaco
Nantes
Guingamp

These were the teams from 2018-19 season. Going into 2019-20, there will likely be a rumbling in the standings. When teams want to win, and when teams strive to win, anything can happen... that's the beauty of each new season.

France's Tournament Guide

The Coupe de France is an expansive tournament available to any professional and amateur teams within France and its territories. The Coupe de la Ligue is for the top three professional leagues within France. The Trophée des Champions is a game in which the winners of Ligue 1 and the Coupe de France come together once a year for a grand showdown.

Top 5 Teams
Paris Saint-Germain
Lille OSC (LOSC)
Lyon
Saint-Etienne
Marseille

PARIS SAINT-GERMAIN

Twitter: @PSG_English
Founded in 1970
Ligue 1 Titles: 8
Coupe de France: 12
Coupe de la Ligue: 8
Trophée des Champions: 8
European Cup and UEFA Champions League: 0
UEFA Super Cup: 0

Known For
Strong attendance
Very passionate fans
Exciting games
Thiago Silva
Zlatan Ibrahimovic
Angel Di Maria
Mbappé
Neymar
Dani Alves
Gianluigi Buffon

A BRIEF TEAM HISTORY

Since it came together as a club in 1970, Paris Saint-Germain (known in some circles as PSG) has won the Ligue 1 title in 1985–86, 1993–94, 2012–13, 2013–14, 2014–15, 2015–16, 2017–18, and 2018-19.

In 2011, things began stirring in Paris. As John Sinnott from *BBC Sport* reported, "Qatar Sports Investments—established in 2005 by son of the Emir and heir to the Qatari throne, Sheikh Tamim Bin Hamad Al Thani—bought a 70% stake in PSG on 30 June and quickly installed former Inter Milan coach Leonardo as general manager."[49]

Since then, the coach has changed and its lineup has become, let's just say, more interesting. Tim Lister from *CNN* reported, "The departure of Neymar from Barcelona to Paris St Germain for a world record fee has it all. A young Brazilian soccer player who came to Europe to seek fame and fortune is offered ludicrous sums to abandon a world-famous club for a Qatari-bankrolled upstart."[50]

It seemed like Neymar had a perfect fit in Barcelona, playing alongside arguably the best passers in the world, with the added firepower of Messi and Luis Suarez up top. It was a Three Musketeers dream come true. Perhaps it was even the most dynamic combination of attacking power in world-club history. How could things be any better? Well, there was speculation that Neymar wanted to be his own man and lead the show (as opposed to sharing center stage with Messi). Interestingly, Neymar's move to PSG had a lot to do with how European soccer has recently been shaped by giant investment groups. "The deal speaks volumes about the almost insane sums of money being thrown at players and clubs in Europe as the continent's transfer market goes into hyper-drive. The influx of cash into European soccer over the past few years has been driven by the Gulf states and (more recently) by China, and by the enormous revenues earned by the top clubs through sponsorship and television rights."[51]

Indeed, big deals have been overtaking the headlines of late. In 2017, Tim Lister provided relevant information pertaining to player movement as it related to Neymar's arrival in Paris. As he wrote, "This time last year, Manchester United set a world record transfer fee when they bought Paul Pogba from Juventus for (the equivalent of) $116 million. Neymar's exercise of his release clause at Barca cost his new employers $263 million."[52]

As it turned out, despite talk of Neymar being a diva and expressing his contempt for the all-around quality of play in France, PSG had a magnificent record in the 2018-19 Ligue 1 season. Alongside Neymar were powerhouses Angel Di Maria, Mbappé, Dani Alves, Thiago Silva, and the renowned Italian keeper, Gianluigi Buffon. In effect, big money has created a new era of winning for PSG, a club that has served as a flagship for billionaire investment strategies, and much more is likely to come.

FACTS ABOUT THEIR CITY

Paris—France's beautiful and legendary capital city—has around 12.5 million people in its metro area. PSG plays in Parc des Princes, a stadium that opened its doors in 1972. It has a capacity of 47,929, but, oddly enough, the largest crowd to view a game came in 1989 with a count of 50,370 when France played Wales, of all teams.

WHERE THE TEAM IS TODAY—
TACTICS AND STRATEGIES

In 2018-19, PSG was seen using a 4-2-2-2 or 3-5-2. French-born keeper Alphonse Areola had a strong presence in goal. Also, within the club would be, of course, the great Gianluigi Buffon, a World Cup champ with Italy and the longtime keeper for Juventus. In front the goal will be a firm defense led by Thiago Silva with midfield and forward contributions coming from numerous angles, including that of Neymar, Mbappé, Angel Di Maria, Edinson Cavani, Marco Verratti, Juan Bernat, and Moussa Diaby.

Both Edinson Cavani (of Uruguay) and Marco Verratti (of Italy) have a lot of experience with PSG and they should be valuable assets moving ahead.

Joining the squad will likely be Timothy Weah (the son of George Weah, the former star with AC Milan and current president of Liberia) who was on loan with Celtic in Scotland. He's a rising star with the US men's national team and will be an interesting development with the club. Will he make big contributions throughout the year? This remains to be seen. It should be noted that he's a talented midfielder with good touch, technique, and instincts, particularly when it comes to passing and combination plays around goal.

Tactics and strategies: Stay consistent and consider the 4-3-3 formation. Without a doubt, the best move for PSG will be to keep up its consistency. While it might be soaring through Ligue 1 at number one, it still needs to respect the lesser teams. If it can stay consistent throughout the season, it should roll through the

223

weaker sides and keep the stronger ones at bay. Perhaps the 4-3-3 would improve things even more for PSG and its quest for the Champions League. It's a formation that puts more pressure on opponents defensively, and offensively more numbers can be used as well. Having Mbappé and a rejuvenated Neymar on the field won't hurt things either. The 4-3-3 would be good for them, and it's a strong formation that enhances consistency.

THOMAS TUCHEL—A BRIEF COACHING PORTRAIT

Thomas Tuchel—who is originally from Germany—comes from the school of Pep Guardiola. Prior to taking the helm at Paris Saint-Germain, Tuchel guided Borussia Dortmund in Germany to good results. Now that he's transitioned westward a bit, one of his biggest challenges may be corralling Neymar, who, by some accounts, is nothing more than a moody diva. Whether this proves to be his biggest test or not, PSG has yet to gather a Champions League title, and such a feat would be truly astounding for the German-born coach. On route to this goal, the 4-2-3-1 may fluctuate at the behest of coach Tuchel, yet, he has a great deal of offensive explosiveness at his disposal, namely Neymar, Angel Di Maria, and Mbappé. Such a wealth of talent is a good place to start for grand visions like conquering Europe's highest club tournament.

KEY PLAYERS AND
THEIR CHARACTERISTICS

Neymar, Mbappé, and Angel Di Maria

Neymar has been fighting injuries throughout his high-profile career, such as a fractured back during World Cup 2014 and a hurt foot going into World Cup 2018. Without the injuries, could he have guided Brazil to a World Cup championship? This may be one of the factors included in the debate about whether Neymar can be considered Brazil's greatest player of all time. The talent is there. However, despite Neymar scoring a remarkable amount of goals for Brazil thus far (60 and counting), he hasn't won a World Cup. Pele, Garrincha, Rivaldo, Ronaldo, and Ronaldinho each gathered the highest trophy for their claim to fame as Brazil's best. Neymar, to his credit, delivered the elusive Olympic gold medal for his country. It was a feat that, oddly enough, hadn't been achieved by Brazil before he pocketed the winning penalty kick against Germany in 2016. Having said that, evidently, similar to his former teammate Messi, Neymar might have to prove his worth in club competition. For now, pushing forward and getting past his injuries, the dazzling dribbler from Brazil is marching forward with PSG after an extremely exciting run during his time in Barcelona, highlighted by a Champions League title from 2014-15. Now that he's vacated the overtly organized passing structure of Barca, a club that may have been his most ideal situation, he has a chance prove his value in world club soccer with PSG which may in fact help cement his case for being one the world's best all-time talents.

Mbappé was a godsend for French fans in Russia 2018 as his brilliant play ledhis team to a second title. Mbappé—who was born in Paris—is hoping to amass several Champions League titles for his home side. To date, the young player has catapulted to stardom, with plenty of goals. It seems like nothing is going to stand in his way during 2019-20, and perhaps a Champions League title is the next milestone for Mbappé.

Angel Di Maria is a relentless left-footed winger who has a knack for driving defenders crazy. He's skinny and crafty and intuitive; he's almost untouchable, an all-time great out wide. The Argentinian talent has recent experience with Manchester United and Real Madrid. He landed with PSG in 2015 and has attained over 110 games and 35 goals so far. Now in his early-thirties, Di Maria might be slowing down a bit, while at the same time, considering his age, he as a lot to prove if he wants to remain an elite player.

Overall Player Rating:
Neymar: 10
Mbappé: 9.9
Angel Di Maria: 9.7

KEY PLAYER STATS

(Total career goals with this club)

	Games Played	Goals
Neymar	34	32
Mbappé	54	43
Angel Di Maria	113	36

WHAT TO WATCH FOR ON TV—HOW MESSI, NEYMAR, RONALDO, AND OTHERS PLAY

During 2018-19, within Ligue 1, there were teams like Dijon FCO, Gulngamp, Caen, Amiens SC, and Monaco, teams that were at the bottom of the standings. Then on the opposite end of the spectrum, you find PSG, soaring in the lead at number one. Some of the reasons, both from the aspect of on-field contributions and locker room leadership, came from the presence of Neymar, Mbappé, Angel Di Maria, Dani Alves, Gianluigi Buffon—all world-class players.

Of late, Mbappé's been surging forward at a ferocious rate, scoring a ton of goals for his age. In fact, he's already attained 50 goals in professional play. And he's only 20 years old! He's off his rocker; he's gone mental; he's one of a kind. All soccer fans should keep their eyes on him as he pumps up the stats, helping PSG to further assert its dominance in France.

In 2018, Vivienne Walt—writing for *TIME*—captured a piece of Mbappé's amazing upward journey: "Mbappé's major stardom began in September last year, when PSG's Qatari owners agreed to pay an astonishing €180 million ($207 million) over five years to the club AS Monaco to transfer Mbappé, its star striker, to his hometown of Paris. They offered to pay him, at the age of 18, a monthly salary of €1.5 million, or about $1.7 million. (PSG will not confirm the figure, widely reported in the French media.) That made Mbappé the most expensive teenager in soccer history at an age when he had just graduated from high school and learned to drive."[53]

This is a salient, trending aspect of modern-day soccer and sports in general around the world. No one can deny that NBA, NFL,

MLB, and soccer salaries have been skyrocketing. (Some say it's out of control and affecting the overall quality of play in a negative way, but that's another story for another day.) PSG has capitalized on bringing what it thinks are the best players possible to Paris to flourish in Parc des Princes. Mbappé, Neymar, Angel Di Maria are historical talents. Legends in their respective positions, and leaders of their generation.

By acquiring such talent, PSG has shelled out the bucks in its favor, which is enhanced by its grand vision of stacking talent in a competitive attempt to keep such players away from traditional landing zones like AC Milan, Juventus, Barcelona, Real Madrid, and Manchester United. PSG wanted to put itself front and center on the map of club soccer royalty, and it has done so. For the time being, anyway. Traditionally, the top-tier talent has been attracted to the aforementioned locations. Will the good times in Paris last? Will a Champions League title be the result? It's very possible. And it's something PSG fans are certainly counting on. Ligue 1 titles are nice, but, in reality, for a club that's spent so much, it's not enough. The conquering of all Europe is next, and PSG is at the forefront of such a quest. This season will be a telling one for its progress, and by season's end, should PSG fall short of a Champions League trophy, things will be very interesting in the next three to five years in terms of potential new recruits.

Currently, as things stand in Ligue 1, PSG is unstoppable; it's a team destined to win the league title and make a run for Champions League glory. LOSC, Lyon, Saint-Etienne, and Marseille were keeping things competitive in 2018-19. Though, by season's end, PSG was out in front. Right now, no one in Ligue 1 can sincerely keep the Parisian giants down. However, once it gets into European competition, its lack of consistency will potentially keep it down. As for now, it's one of the most stacked teams in terms of talent, and any true fan should want to view each and every game as PSG weaves its way through a campaign that could in fact be absolutely brilliant.

WHAT ARE THEIR CHANCES OF WINNING THE LEAGUE TITLE THIS YEAR?

Extremely high. Excellent. It's more a question of who will stop PSG?

Overall Team Ranking: 9.3-9.6

LILLE OSC (LOSC)

Twitter: @LOSC_EN
Founded in 1944
Ligue 1 Titles: 3
Coupe de France: 6
Coupe de la Ligue: 0
Trophée des Champions: 0
European Cup and UEFA Champions League: 0
UEFA Super Cup: 0

Known For
Strong attendance
Very passionate fans
Exciting games
Marceau Somerlinck
Jean Baratte
Andre Strappe
Luiz Araújo
Loïc Rémy
Nicolas Pépé
Thiago Mendes

A BRIEF TEAM HISTORY

Lille OSC—which is typically known as LOSC—was founded back in 1944 at the close of WWII. To its credit, LOSC won the Ligue 1 title on three occasions in 1945-46, 1953-54, and 2010-11. And that's not it. LOSC also won the Coupe de France in 1945-46, 1946-47, 1947-48, 1952-53, 1954-55, and 2010-11. Notwithstanding the acquisition of lesser competitions, LOSC has not won the UEFA Champions League. Perhaps this is a trophy that will someday find its way to Lille. For now, it's a team that has been doing very well in Ligue 1. It has a strong lineup, and the goal is to outdo Paris Saint-Germain.

FACTS ABOUT THEIR CITY

Lille—which is located way up in the north of France—has a particular vibe about it. Corinne Labalme of *The New York Times* wrote, "Lille was ruled by Burgundy and Spain until Louis XIV of France captured it in 1667. Dollhouse-style 17th- and 18th-century brick townhouses in the city center give the metropolis a small-town flavor, but this dynamic city has nearly one million people when its satellites—Roubaix, Villeneuve d'Ascq and Tourcoing—are counted."[54] Say what you will about art and fashion being centralized in Paris, over the years Lille has continued to be an alluring outpost for fashion design and interior design. of the city is also home to a well-known flea market.

Beyond the streets of trade, the world of soccer looms large in the form of Stade Pierre-Mauroy—the stadium LOSC uses—which adds architectural beauty to the area. It's very new structure, having opened in 2012.

WHERE THE TEAM IS TODAY—TACTICS AND STRATEGIES

Last season, LOSC was seen using a 4-2-3-1, with contributions from Xeka, Thiago Mendes, Jonathan Ikoné, Jonathan Bamba, Nicolas Pépé, and Luiz Araújo, along with Loïc Rémy and Rafael Leão up top.

Tactics and strategies: Keep the momentum going and use outside backs in the attack more often.

Keeping momentum going is a tough request for many teams. It suggests that, one, the momentum might fall off, and, two, if momentum declines, then the whole season is a disaster. These things don't necessarily have to be true. In fact, momentum is a tricky term altogether. Some believe in it wholeheartedly, while others think it's a distraction, a mystical state of mind that cons players into thinking that what they're doing is right. However the argument unfolds, it can't be denied: Momentum in sports is a real thing. At least we think so. Maybe it is just in the mind, a dream-like state in which nothing really exists.

As for using outside backs in the attack more often, it would be advantageous for LOSC to explore this venture and delineate a plan for the outside backs to get involved more often in terms of dribbling near goal and unleashing shots on goal. Such influences for this type of attack would come in the form of Brazilian national team defenders of yore, like Jorginho, Cafu, and Roberto Carlos. It should go without saying that LOSC and its staff members are aware of such an approach (one would hope so, anyway), and this is not an attempt to claim anyone failed in this regard. However, given the unbelievable results from last season, it would be in LOSC's best interest to examine a revitalized approach in this department as it might just put the club over the top.

CHRISTOPHE GALTIER—
A BRIEF COACHING PORTRAIT

Christophe Galtier is a French-born coach and former defender with LOSC, Marseille, and a few teams. Last season, during 2018-19, coach Galtier showed a propensity for a 4-2-3-1. It wouldn't be surprising to see a 4-4-2 tossed into the mix either. In any case, last season was a good one. Should coach Galtier stipulate an agreement in his contract to stay longer with the club, he certainly would have room to grow with the progress built upon to this point. At this juncture, a plan to improve things, with all eyes on the Ligue 1 championship, is unfolding. Though, as anyone should rightfully know, PSG is standing in the way. It would seem that no matter what coach Galtier does, it might not be enough to achieve first place. PSG has a team full of superstars, and this is the very thing that LOSC lacks. Perhaps Galtier has done all he can with the talent at hand? Perhaps a few big trades are in the works? Fans should know that *every* ounce of success cannot be the responsibility of the coach. Sometimes coaches can only do so much with a certain group of talent. Despite the roster lacking a true global superstar, it's a good, solid team. Right now, Galtier and LOSC are on the verge of something special. Big moves in terms of trades may happen soon, and fans of the club would certainly welcome a few key pieces in the roster for that extra push forward.

KEY PLAYERS AND
THEIR CHARACTERISTICS

Thiago Mendes, Jonathan Bamba, Loïc Rémy, and Nicolas Pépé

Thiago Mendes—who was born in 1992 in Brazil—is a midfielder who's played over 50 games with LOSC so far. As someone who isn't the biggest goal-scorer, his role is to organize and orchestrate things for the more prominent attacking players. It will be his job, as it was in the previous season, to perpetuate connectivity in the midfield, with, as fans are continuing to count on, a nuanced Brazilian touch. While he's not quite as technically sound as Ever Banega or Luka Modric, he still brings a little something the table, and fans should look forward to interesting games with Mendes on the field.

Jonathan Bamba played a number of games with Saint-Etienne before arriving in Lille. He also has a good deal of youth national team experience with France. Bamba will have a great deal of expectations placed on him in the midfield this season. As a younger player (born in 1996), he's getting into his mid-twenties, and room for growth with the club will have limitations as supporters are looking forward to toppling league leaders PSG. As a result, Bamba and company will need to step up and make a difference if LOSC has any hope of reaching first place.

Loïc Rémy is a multifaceted attacking player with experience on the French national team. He's a bit of a journeyman with clubs, and he's had stops in Lyon, Nice, Marseille, and Chelsea, to name a few. Should he remain with LOSC, he'll be adding a great deal of depth to the frontline attack.

Nicolas Pépé was born in France, though he plays for the national team of Ivory Coast. Found on Lille's wing, he's acquired over 60 games with a salient feature to his game: an astounding 30 goals thus far. He's racking them up. Fans are looking forward to a lot more production from the young player born in 1995.

Overall Player Rating:
Thiago Mendes: 8
Jonathan Bamba: 8
Loïc Rémy: 8.8
Nicolas Pépé: 8.9

KEY PLAYER STATS

(Total career goals with this club)

	Games Played	Goals
Thiago Mendes	52	3
Jonathan Bamba	32	11
Loïc Rémy	15	3
Nicolas Pépé	69	32

WHAT TO WATCH FOR ON TV—HOW MESSI, NEYMAR, RONALDO, AND OTHERS PLAY

Heading into the final stretch of the 2018-19 season, LOSC had a 3-2 win over Nantes on March 31, 2019, followed by a 1-1 tie with Stade Reims on April 7, 2019. LOSC was firmly making a claim for second place, behind PSG. On April 14, 2019, *The Washington Post* reported on a big win that LOSC had over

Paris Saint-Germain: "PSG's defense was unable to contain outstanding Lille forward Nicolas Pepe, who scored the second goal and set up the fourth and fifth to underline Lille's brilliant teamwork."[55]

This tumbled into a finish that was far superior than the rest of Ligue 1 but not enough to overtake PSG. Building on this momentum, LOSC has a lot of energy moving into the 2019-20 season. Loïc Rémy and Rafael Leão can ensure a strong billing. Will it be able to run PSG out of first place? This is a tricky question. It probably won't happen. However, if someone is going to do it, then look no further than LOSC. With the help of Thiago Mendes, Jonathan Bamba, and Nicolas Pépé, along with Xeka and Luiz Araújo, taking down PSG might end up being a reality.

WHAT ARE THEIR CHANCES OF WINNING THE LEAGUE TITLE THIS YEAR?

The chances for LOSC are good. Very good. But it might take a lot of good fortune to overcome the high-end talent pool of Paris Saint-Germain.

Overall Team Ranking: 9.1

LYON
(OLYMPIQUE LYONNAIS)

Twitter: @OL, @OL_English
Founded in 1950
Ligue 1 Titles: 7
Coupe de France: 5
Coupe de la Ligue: 1
Trophée des Champions: 8
European Cup and UEFA Champions League: 0
UEFA Super Cup: 0

Known For
Dominating Ligue 1 in the 2000s
Passionate fans
Exciting games
Juninho
Michael Essien
Florent Malouda
Karim Benzema
Lisandro Lopez
Alexandre Lacazette

A BRIEF TEAM HISTORY

Lyon—officially known as Olympique Lyonnais—dates back to 1950, and it has brought in a few significant league trophies from the 1960s and 70s. Then a larger sequence of events occurred which makes one wonder: Who says Lyon hasn't left a path of dominance in France since 2000? This is a club that won Ligue 1 in 2001-02, 2002-03, 2003-04, 2004-05, 2005-06, 2006-07, 2007-08, thus earning a Juventus-esque reverence in France. It's as if Lyon said, "That's it, this league is ours. Enough is enough." Then, as it's commonly said, "All good things must end."

Lyon might not have won the European Cup (back when it was called that) or the UEFA Champions League (as it's called today), but crazier things have happened. Look at Leicester City and everything it accomplished. In respect to taking the Champions League title, Lyon could theoretically re-enact the big splash Leicester City made in the Premier League with its own move on the Champions League title. Sure, Leicester City didn't win Europe's grand prize, but it shook the world, that's for sure. In terms of the Champions League title, Lyon can be compared with Leicester City as a club that just might rise up and do the unthinkable. Who's to say Lyon might never go one further and find its way into the Champions League history books? It's a long shot, but it's worth a try. And who knows, it might just work out after all. Keep in mind, Lyon has an unbelievably large amount of league success. But nonetheless, if Lyon can translate Leicester City's Premier League success to Europe's biggest tournament, then a true place in history would be irrefutable.

Recently, a clear avenue for Lyon to navigate its way to Ligue 1 superiority has become a bit roadblocked. One might think that

PSG alone would qualify as a *bête noire* for Lyon, but, given the competitive race for the top of the pack in Ligue 1, it could be successfully argued that LOSC, Saint-Etienne, Marseille, and Stade Reims could also qualify as worthy candidates for such a title. In fact, this list of teams is a strong group of competitors that stand between Lyon and the fairytale-like run that it had in the 2000s. Yet, it's a challenge that makes it worth donning a jersey, which the fans—such as a well-known Bad Gones, which formed in 1987—live and breathe for.

FACTS ABOUT THEIR CITY

Lyon has around 2.2 million people in the metro area. Games for Lyon are held in the Parc Olympique Lyonnais—also known as Groupama Stadium—which has a little over 100 suites available for use and holds approximately 59,000 people. Looking for a local wine venue? Cave Bataillon would be an option to drop by possibly before a game or after a game or both.

WHERE THE TEAM IS TODAY— TACTICS AND STRATEGIES

As for Lyon's dream of someday winning the Champions League, this may in fact be a lofty endeavor, a challenge sure to be met with fierce opposition at every corner. In fact, Lyon got pretty far in 2018-19 during which it made it all the way to the Round of 16 where it lost to Barcelona. Not bad company.

Tactics and strategies: Probably stick with the 4-3-3.

During the 2018-19 season, some of Lyon's formations may have come across as arbitrary. It was seen using a 4-2-3-1, 4-1-2-1-2, and 4-3-3. Frankly, the 4-1-2-1-2 seems a little complicated. Though, essentially the 4-1-2-1-2 is nothing more than a 4-3-3 disguised as Woody Allen. When it comes down to it, the 4-3-3 is the most effective formation available. This is certainly an opinion-based observation and one that others certainly would argue against. Still, formations are dependent on how players play in them, which, in turn, is dependent on how players have been coached. Having said that, the 4-3-3 provides great defensive pressure which can be applied all over the field. Offensively, it connects players well, as most areas on the field are covered. The 4-2-3-1 provides a sense of balance. It's not the worst formation in the world, though a 4-3-3 would perhaps be a better option for Lyon.

A few players featured last year include Nabil Fekir, Lucas Tousart, Martin Terrier, Houssem Aouar, Moussa Dembélé, Bertrand Traoré, and Rafael, an outside defender who has spent some time on the field with Brazil and previously played with Manchester United. Can this group, along with it's strong supporting cast, be abled to improve upon last season's results? A lot is riding on the 2019-20 season. Fekir, who has World Cup experience, will be expected to commandeer center stage in midfield and guide the team—which features a few young players, including Tousart and Aouar—to a higher level, thus achieving bigger and better results.

BRUNO GENESIO—A BRIEF
COACHING PORTRAIT

Bruno Genesio—who was born in 1966 in Lyon, France—represents his hometown as coach after playing for Lyon as a midfielder in the 1980s and 90s. He began his command of the team back in 2015 and brought excellent results during 2018-19 as the club achieved a place in the Round of 16 during its pursuit of Champions League glory. His team's loss to Barcelona should prove a strong lesson while also instilling a fervent desire to get back and have another go at it.

KEY PLAYERS AND
THEIR CHARACTERISTICS

Nabil Fekir, Moussa Dembélé, and Memphis Depay

Nabil Fekir—the club's current captain—has played more than 135 games and is pushing 60 goals for Lyon. Fekir—who was born in 1993—is also a French international who participated in the 2018 World Cup run. Considering his experiences with club and country, the attacking midfielder has a great deal of responsibility to guide Lyon in a winning direction this year.

Moussa Dembélé—who was born in 1996 in France—has made quite an impression with Lyon since his arrival in 2018. Dembélé got an early start in pro soccer, first with Fulham and then with Celtic. In both cases, he tallied up a good amount of goals. Thus far, he's gone over 10 goals with Lyon and is definitely looking for more. The young French forward has a lot of pressure riding on his every move now, and a big season could be in the making.

Memphis Depay didn't quite get the goal production at Manchester United that he wanted, though he's stepped up in Lyon as a significant scoring threat with 30 and counting. He provides speed and determination around goal. Certainly, the Dutch forward has a lot more in the tank with strong runs and thoughtful and skilled play.

Overall Player Rating:
Nabil Fekir: 9
Moussa Dembélé: 8.9
Memphis Depay: 8.9

KEY PLAYER STATS

(Total career goals with this club)

	Games Played	Goals
Nabil Fekir	136	54
Moussa Dembélé	27	12
Memphis Depay	80	30

WHAT TO WATCH FOR ON TV—HOW MESSI, NEYMAR, RONALDO, AND OTHERS PLAY

Nabil Fekir, Moussa Dembélé, and Memphis Depay, along with a strong supporting cast, comprise a formidable attack.

Bertrand Traoré is definitely a player for opponents to watch out for; with Lyon he's compiled over 55 games and 20 goals to date. Adding more depth to the roster are two young French players: Martin Terrier, an attacking player to keep an eye on, and Houssem Aouar, a midfielder who has put in over 50 games to date along with a handful of goals.

Based on the results from 2018-19 season, which were good, there is a strong impetus to grasp a ton of wins in 2019-20 with an eye on the Champions League down the road. During the Champions League run of 2018-19, Lyon advanced from Group F, which included Manchester City, Shakhtar Donetsk, and 1899 Hoffenheim. Then Lyon suffered a tough loss to Barcelona in the Round of 16.

As a result, it has had some time to regroup, and Lyon will be fielding a team of players hungry for goals, wins, and a high level of success. It's a team that has gotten a taste, and it's looking forward to much more.

According to Dr. Sanjay Gupta, speaking with Anderson Cooper on *CNN* on April 12, 2019, some people in Japan are "bathing in the forest," which refers to a practice of breathing in the forest air which, according to complicated scientific research, delivers stress-relieving chemicals (which the trees use to protect themselves) that human receptors apparently gather to confront stress. Perhaps a similar process will take place as the fans of Lyon send good vibes to the players with the result transcending greatness.

WHAT ARE THEIR CHANCES OF WINNING THE LEAGUE TITLE THIS YEAR?

Quite good. Better than most in the high end of the standings.

Overall Team Ranking: 9.2

SAINT-ETIENNE

Twitter: @ASSEofficiel
Founded in 1919
Ligue 1 Titles: 10
Coupe de France: 6
Coupe de la Ligue: 1
Trophée des Champions: 5
European Cup and UEFA Champions League: 0
UEFA Super Cup: 0

Known For
Stade Geoffroy-Guichard
Passionate fans
Exciting games
Hervé Revelli
Michel Platini
Wahbi Khazri
Yann M'Vila
Arnaud Nordin

A BRIEF TEAM HISTORY

Overall, Saint-Etienne—also known as AS Saint-Etienne—has done well in league play, and it took first place in Ligue 1 in 1956-57, 1963-64, 1966-67, 1967-68, 1968-69, 1969-70, 1973-74, 1974-75, 1975-76, and 1980-81. The good times didn't stop there. Saint-Etienne has also won the Coupe de France in 1961-62, 1967-68, 1969-70, 1973-74, 1974-75, and 1976-77. Furthermore, it had a good run with the Trophée des Champions, taking first place in 1957, 1962, 1967, 1968, and 1969. In essence, the 1960s and 70s were good for Saint-Etienne within France, not to mention 1979-82 during Michel Platini's time at the club. Without a doubt, Platini would be the club's most prominent player. After his run with Saint-Etienne, France's former captain and European Cup champ moved on to Juventus where he won the Ballon d'Or three years in a row. He's considered one of soccer's all-time great players. As for his time as president of UEFA, don't ask. However, just as Santos will always be associated with Pele, any club that's had a great player walk through its halls will always be looked upon with a touch of reverence, and Platini's experience with Saint-Etienne will definitely be the same.

Outside of France, on its quest for European glory, Saint-Etienne came close to winning the European Cup back in 1975-76 as it earned placed second after losing to Bayern Munich in the final by a score of 1-0.

The 2018-19 Ligue 1 season was fairly good for Saint-Etienne as it huddled around fifth place, coexisting with other contenders—including LOSC, Lyon, and Marseille—that were chasing the leaders, PSG. True, Saint-Etienne was not low in the rankings, like Guingamp or Dijon FCO, but it needs to thrive this season with new energy to improve and return to its glory days.

FACTS ABOUT THEIR CITY

Saint-Etienne has a population of approximately 178,000 people, and, geographically speaking, it's in an interesting location; it's as though it wants to be in the southeastern portion of France, but a little central. AS Saint-Etienne's stadium, Stade Geoffroy-Guichard, kicked things off back in 1931, and it's had plenty of renovations since. During the 1998 World Cup, it hosted a classic game between England and Argentina, which, following a 2-2 draw, ended in a victory for Argentina in a penalty shootout.

WHERE THE TEAM IS TODAY— TACTICS AND STRATEGIES

You'll likely see a 4-2-3-1 or possibly a 3-4-1-2. As these formations were used in 2018-19, the team will likely continue down this route. If one were to choose one over the other, it would make the most sense to ditch the 3-4-1-2 and go with the 4-2-3-1. Why? It would probably be in Saint-Etienne's best interest to find balance with four defenders as opposed to three (this is largely the case in terms of possession). A few players from last season were Rémy Cabella, Wahbi Khazri, Arnaud Nordin, Robert Berić, Yann M'Vila, Romain Hamouma, Gabriel Silva, Neven Subotić, William Saliba, Stéphane Ruffier, and Mathieu Debuchy. It was a lineup of mostly French talent. For Saint-Etienne fans, the overall result was good, bordering on very good, but the Ligue 1 title was far out of reach. We're not talking about Guingamp or Dijon FCO here, but they were still incapable of gaining the title.

Tactics and strategies: improve possession and the two-man game.

For any team around the world, possession is potentially a lost cause. Teams like Bayern Munich, Real Madrid, and Barcelona tend to excel because of elite talent, and, not to mention, a shrewd eye for elite possession play. In order for possession to work at the highest level, the two-man game is crucial. For those unfamiliar with the concept of the two-man game, it's rather simple. If Claude passes to William and if William passes the ball right back to Claude, then the two-man game has occurred. It sounds simple, easily dismissed, but at its core the concept is profound. In essence, Saint-Etienne should increase its two-man game combinations. This is not to say that Saint-Etienne has completely ignored its possession play. However, should Saint-Etienne improve in this area and increase two-man game combinations, then its overall possession game will drastically improve, and, unsurprisingly, more goals should occur down the road. After all, at this point, Saint-Etienne doesn't have any global superstar talent on its squad to push the organization over the top. Therefore, a strong team-first approach, with an improvement in the possession department, is the best road to success. Using elite possession play should be Saint-Etienne's secret weapon.

Hold on. I've focused on possession while still insinuating Saint-Etienne is down and out. Far from it. Saint-Etienne is definitely not down and out. Yet. Before you rule out Saint-Etienne, consider this. To win Ligue 1, not only will it have to get through the teams ranked 12th and 13th ranked, but it will also have to surpass the mighty PSG. At the moment, the latter is a standard that might be too much for any team in Ligue 1 to live up to. Although, coach Jean-Louis Gasset might have other ideas.

JEAN-LOUIS GASSET— A BRIEF COACHING PORTRAIT

Jean-Louis Gasset was born in 1953 in Montpellier, France. He eventually played midfield for his hometown team from 1975-85. He coached there as well. Along with other coaching stops, he was an assistant for France. Now he has the reigns of Saint-Etienne, a club with promise and potential. One lingering question: How long will he remain at the helm of Les Verts? He's done well, but let's face it: Saint-Etienne is not PSG. How much of this falls on the coach? That's a question for the ages. It might be an easy out to let him go in favor of a new leader, one that could improve the club's chances of dethroning Ligue 1's mega club. Or owners could stay with Gasset and see how far he takes it. We'll have to wait and see. For now, the club is in his hands, and anything's possible.

KEY PLAYERS AND THEIR CHARACTERISTICS

Wahbi Khazri, Yann M'Vila, and Arnaud Nordin

Wahbi Khazri was born in France. He represents Tunisia's national team, having gained over 40 caps to date. Since his arrival in Saint-Etienne back in 2018, the attacking force of Khazri has already delivered more than 10 goals, and he's certainly looking for more. He's a valuable asset for the club, but with that comes responsibility. His task will be to get Saint-Etienne out in front of LOSC, Lyon, Marseille, and, of course, the big dog on the block, PSG. Is he up to the task? That's for Khazri to figure out, but drawing on energy from the fans, he'll have every opportunity to prove his worth.

Yann M'Vila—who was born in 1990 in France—is a defensive midfielder who holds the fort with tenacity and organization. He might not be a goal-scoring threat, but he brings experience from the French national team with him.

Arnaud Nordin—a French-born striker—has a lot of pressure to build upon his previous season as a younger player still making his way in the league. He's already managed to gain valuable experience with AS Nancy and Saint-Etienne, as well as time within the French youth national team system. He's a player on the rise, and, in the next few years, his time with Saint-Etienne will be crucial for the club and his growth as an individual talent.

Overall Player Rating:
Wahbi Khazri: 9
Yann M'Vila: 8.8
Arnaud Nordin: 8

KEY PLAYER STATS

(Total career goals with this club)

	Games Played	Goals
Wahbi Kharzri	19	12
Yann M'Vila	36	0
Arnaud Nordin	15	2

WHAT TO WATCH FOR ON TV—HOW MESSI, NEYMAR, RONALDO, AND OTHERS PLAY

Much of the focus for the season will be on Wahbi Khazri, Yann M'Vila, and Arnaud Nordin. But you can't forget Robert Berić. A member of Slovenia's national team he is definitely an asset to the team. He's scored 20 goals to date, and he should be an important part of the attack moving forward.

Will a mantra of "Obtenons la quatrième place" echo throughout the locker room? Well, likely the players, along with the fans and team owners, will want much more than fourth place. Though, as the season moves forward, a third- or second-place finish for Saint-Etienne might be out of reach. It's a highly talented club with a chance to move ahead of Lyon, LOSC, and PSG, though not without a lot of luck. For now, anyway, the club will have to settle for a good year that does not end with a glorious hoisting of the Ligue 1 trophy or qualification into the Champions League. That's almost guaranteed. But with a few clever trades—a move here and there, such as the acquisition of Neymar and Angel Di Maria (which will never happen)—Saint-Etienne might find itself in a better position for ultimate success in the next five years.

WHAT ARE THEIR CHANCES OF WINNING THE LEAGUE TITLE THIS YEAR?

Platini has a better chance of being reinstated as president of UEFA than Saint-Etienne's chances of winning Ligue 1 in 2019-20. Although, I suppose anything is possible.

Overall Team Ranking: 8.6

MARSEILLE

Twitter: @OM_English
Founded in 1899
Ligue 1 Titles: 9
Coupe de France: 10
Coupe de la Ligue: 3
Trophée des Champions: 3
European Cup and UEFA Champions League: 1
UEFA Super Cup: 0

Known For
Passionate fans
Exciting games
Josip Skoblar
Jean-Pierre Papin
Didier Drogba
Samir Nasri
Franck Ribéry
Dimitri Payet
Morgan Sanson
Florian Thauvin
Maxime Lopez

A BRIEF TEAM HISTORY

Marseille is a club that has been there and done that. Since its founding back in 1899, it's had plenty of good times over the years. It won the Ligue 1 title in 1936-37, 1947-48, 1970-71, 1971-72, 1988-89, 1989-90, 1990-91, 1991-92, and 2009-10.

That's not all. It also won the Coupe de France in 1923-24, 1925-26, 1926-27, 1934-35, 1937-38, 1942-43, 1968-69, 1971-72, 1975-76, and 1988-89.

It won the Coupe de la Ligue in 2009-10, 2010-11, and 2011-12.

And let's not forget when Marseille won its first and only UEFA Champions League title in 1992-93 after defeating AC Milan in the final.

Jean-Pierre Papin—a goal-scoring French striker—won the Ballon d'Or in 1991 while playing for Marseille.

For the past couple of years, Marseille has hovered around fourth and fifth place in Ligue 1. This is good news and—certainly—bad news. It's never great to finish in "fourth;" however, Marseille has certainly avoided the bottom of the standings, which is the good news. It's been consistently slightly above average. But Marseille now wants to improve and push its way into the top tier of Ligue 1, where it's definitely been before.

FACTS ABOUT THEIR CITY

Located on the Mediterranean in southeastern France, Marseille has a population of around 1.8 million people in the metro area. Is it a dangerous city? Some may say so. Anthony Bourdain paid Marseille a visit for *Anthony Bourdain: Parts Unknown*—which aired on *CNN*—and he illustrated how Marseille is definitely a culturally diverse place. Despite its proclivity for crime, soccer would be the biggest event in town, and locals love their team. Stade Vélodrome, Marseille's stadium, holds around 67,000 people. It's a place tucked away on the coastal border of France, a big city on the Mediterranean close to Italy, Corsica, Sardinia, and Spain. This is where Marseille's people come together, to celebrate life, cheer on their team, and get lost in the beautiful game.

WHERE THE TEAM IS TODAY—TACTICS AND STRATEGIES

Marseille was seen using a 4-2-3-1 or 4-4-2 last season, and a few players featured in 2018-19 were Dimitri Payet, Lucas Ocampos, Morgan Sanson, Nemanja Radonjić,

Mario Balotelli, Kevin Strootman, Luiz Gustavo, Florian Thauvin, Maxime Lopez, Valère Germain, Steve Mandanda, and Hiroki Sakai. Better than most teams in Ligue 1, Marseille stood its ground around the fifth-place position in the standings.

Tactics and strategies: spend more money, acquire better talent, and improve chemistry on the field.

If this is done, Marseille won't find itself in fifth place, or close to it, at the close of the 2019-20 season. Presumably, changing little things here and there will improve its chances within Ligue 1 in 2020-21 and beyond. After all, something has to be done. It's clearly being held back by something. It can certainly get more out of Payet, Sanson, and Strootman. There's a lot that can be done, yet average isn't going to get Marseille much further than the unexciting and familiar fifth place.

RUDI GARCIA—A BRIEF COACHING PORTRAIT

Rudi Garcia—a French native who has previously coached Roma, LOSC, and Dijon FCO—has a wealth of knowledge to draw on, along with a number of high-profile players at his disposal, including Dimitri Payet and Mario Balotelli. But getting Marseille out of fourth and fifth place of Ligue 1 might be trickier than first appears when you have PSG, LOSC, and Lyon waiting in the wings. His former team—LOSC—had a strong season in 2018-19, upping the bar of success. Some think Marseille's return to glory is but a step or two away. Garcia has every intention of making that dream a reality.

KEY PLAYERS AND THEIR CHARACTERISTICS

Dimitri Payet, Morgan Sanson, Florian Thauvin, and Maxime Lopez

Dimitri Payet is sensational, creative midfielder who keeps defenses on their guard with his ability to create a shot from sheer solo brilliance. He's quick, assertive, thoughtful, skillful, and dangerous around goal. Payet, who is always a pleasure to watch, is a player to build around, and Marseille is looking to get plenty of results from this talented player.

Morgan Sanson—who was born in 1994 in France—has represented French youth national teams (U19 and U21). The midfielder is usually found in the center of the field, connecting teammates with passes, pushing the tempo of the game to his advantage. Since his arrival in Marseille, he's gathered over 10 goals. His arrival in Marseille followed a short move from Montpellier; so short a distance he could've theoretically gotten there by a cheap Uber ride. As he's settled in, the club has done well (in a universe where "well" equates to "average"). In fact, despite Marseille doing much better than the lower half of clubs in Ligue 1, it still has a lot of room for improvement, and Sanson is front and center as a young veteran on the team. Many fans will be relying on his constructive play in midfield, and the pressure is on to deliver and make Marseille a true contender in French soccer.

Florian Thauvin was born in 1993 in France. He's represented the French national team and scored more than 60 goals with Marseille. The prolific scorer is ready for more and eager to take on Ligue 1 in 2019-20.

So far, **Maxime Lopez** has spent his professional career with Marseille. The young midfielder, who was born in 1997, might not be a big scorer, but he's racking up a lot of playing time and entering the realm of being a young veteran talent.

Overall Player Rating:
Dimitri Payet: 9.2
Morgan Sanson: 8.8
Florian Thauvin: 8.9
Maxime Lopez: 8.4

KEY PLAYER STATS

(Total career goals with this club)

	Games Played	Goals
Dimitri Payet	143	29
Morgan Sanson	78	14
Florian Thauvin	184	65
Maxime Lopez	78	4

WHAT TO WATCH FOR ON TV—HOW MESSI, NEYMAR, RONALDO, AND OTHERS PLAY

Dimitri Payet is a dynamic attacking player, one who will guide things going forward. He might just be the most salient star on Marseille. Even still, Marseille lacks the star power that PSG has to its advantage. Morgan Sanson is a great example of a good player, a solid one at that. However, he's a midfielder who inevitably creates opportunities for star players. He's not a star in the same way Neymar and Mbappé are, and never will be. Having said that, Marseille would benefit from making a huge trade to acquire a massive star. However, such a thing seems unlikely right now. In the meantime, Marseille has Payet, who is definitely a player to build play around. Florian Thauvin has scored a ton of goals and is also a great asset.

Mario Balotelli—who was formerly a star in Serie A—made an impression with his goal-scoring ability, and he could be an influential presence for Marseille this season. Will Balotelli remain a member of the club? It's a good question. He's bounced around a bit, and it wouldn't be surprising to see him traded. Valère Germain should be a viable option up top. There are interesting components in the Marseille camp. It's a team to be reckoned with, no doubt about it.

This is a club—one of past success—that is going to play full throttle in a full-on attempt to gain a foothold in the upper echelon of the Ligue 1 standings. In 2018-19, Marseille did well, placing fairly high, that is, compared to Guingamp. Marseille also did much better than Monaco and Toulouse. Though, without a doubt, Marseille was not about to topple PSG.

Things could change. This could be the year. Then again, 36 years could go by, and Marseille might still be a side that's better than average, with less than average tendencies, languishing near the top but not quite in first place—which is where Marseille is today. Marseille, though, seems to have something building in the works. As of 2019-20, Marseille is a team looking for something greater than last year. Can it push everyone else aside and take first place in Ligue 1? It would be glib to fully support such idea notion. It's possible, though it's unlikely, and Marseille will probably end up around fifth yet again.

WHAT ARE THEIR CHANCES OF WINNING THE LEAGUE TITLE THIS YEAR?

Not exactly great.

Overall Team Ranking: 8.5

THE UNDERDOGS

Bordeaux
OGC Nice

BORDEAUX

Twitter: @girondins
Founded in 1881
Ligue 1 Titles: 6
Coupe de France: 4
Coupe de la Ligue: 3
Trophée des Champions: 3
European Cup and UEFA Champions League: 0
UEFA Super Cup: 0

A QUICK GLANCE

Keep an eye on Bordeaux. It didn't have the best of times in 2018-19, but it finished better off than other clubs. True, its chances of taking down PSG are slim, if not completely nil. Is Bordeaux going to win the league championship? Absolutely not. For Bordeaux to do such a thing it would take a fairytale-like miracle and then some. It's not in the club's DNA to win it all at this point, and it probably won't be for the next five years, at least. And, even at that point it's questionable. It needs to restructure a lot of things to get there; it's just not the team right now. However, it has some players of interest, including François

Kamano, Zaydou Youssouf, Otávio, and Toma Bašić. These guys might pull off some magic and get Bordeaux into a top five position. Plenty of others will certainly step up as well. Bordeaux might have a few tricks up its sleeve, and it'll definitely make for an interesting season.

Overall Team Ranking: 7.4

OGC NICE

Twitter: @ogcnice_eng
Founded in 1904
Ligue 1 Titles: 4
Coupe de France: 3
Coupe de la Ligue: 0
Trophée des Champions: 0
European Cup and UEFA Champions League: 0
UEFA Super Cup: 0

A QUICK GLANCE

OGC Nice is another club to watch, one that has an opportunity to improve upon last season and get into the top five this time around. In reality though, it's a club that has a chance to make a few waves in Ligue 1 during 2019-20, but no one will be surprised if it lands somewhere in the middle. With a few players in place, including Allan Saint-Maximin, Youcef Attal, Bassem Srarfi, and Adrien Tameze, it just might turn things around and shock a few people.

Overall Team Ranking: 8.2

PREDICTIONS FOR 2019-20 SEASON

ENGLAND
PREMIER LEAGUE

How will the Premier League play out in 2019-20? In first place will be Liverpool. In second will be Manchester City. (However, Manchester City could just as easily be in first, with Liverpool in second.) Third will go to Tottenham. Chelsea will secure fourth place. Manchester United will outdo Arsenal for fifth. So, therefore, sixth will go to Arsenal. Who will be close behind? Lingering will be Wolverhampton, Everton, Watford, Leicester City. Following them, well, a lot could happen. You'll have West Ham, Crystal Palace, Newcastle, and a few others. Not to leave them out, but really? Are they really going to make a convincing run for the top 10? It's doubtful. Speaking on behalf of those teams, it's unlikely Southampton will break into the top 10, so there you go. One team worth extra consideration for big things in 2019-20 is Wolverhampton. There have been some interesting developments in the club recently, and while they may not immediately lead to a first-place finish, big results could be coming soon. Who will be the biggest scorer?

There are many great goal-scorers, but perhaps none more so than Mo Salah. True, many are worthy of the scoring title, including Harry Kane, Sadio Mane, and Sergio Aguero. Those are a few of the great ones, but, at this time in the Premier League, my prediction lies with Mo Salah. Expect Salah—the exceptional Egyptian goal machine—to win the league's scoring title.

(1) Liverpool
(2) Manchester City
(3) Tottenham
(4) Chelsea
(5) Manchester United

GERMANY
BUNDESLIGA

How on earth would someone not pick Bayern Munich to win the 2019-20 season? Oh, that's right: Borussia Dortmund. Dortmund is the one team that poses a serious threat for number one in the Bundesliga, outside of maybe RB Leipzig, Eintracht, and Monchengladbach (a big maybe on the last two). It was a tight race for number one between Bayern Munich and Borussia Dortmund in 2018-19. Though, for 2019-20, I'm going with Bayern Munch in first place, Borussia Dortmund in second, RB Leipzig in third, Bayer Leverkusen in fourth, and Eintracht in fifth. Very close to the fifth place position will be Monchengladbach, Hoffenheim, Werder, Wolfsburg and possibly Fortuna. Though I wouldn't count on Fortuna getting much done. The same goes for Hertha, Mainz, and SC Freiburg.

Robert Lewandowski will likely be the leading scorer. Though, watch out for Timo Werner who just might surpass Lewandowski for the title.

(1) Bayern Munich
(2) Borussia Dortmund
(3) RB Leipzig
(4) Bayer Leverkusen
(5) Eintracht Frankfurt

SPAIN
LA LIGA

La Liga is an interesting league to predict. With the return of Zinedine Zidane as coach of Real Madrid, it's not hard to favor his side. After all, with Zidane as coach, Real Madrid won three Champions League titles in a row. And that just happened! Now he's back. With his leadership on the sideline, I predict Real Madrid wins La Liga, with Barcelona in a close second, and Atletico Madrid following up in third. However, this isn't to say that Real Madrid will have an easy time of it. In fact, I wouldn't be surprised if Zidane and company finish in second or third. I imagine a few trades are in the works at Real Madrid, big trades, and it may take a year to get things flowing in the direction that Zidane wants. However, that's just my disclaimer. I do predict that right away Real Madrid will take first place. In fourth will be Getafe, in fifth will be Sevilla, and in sixth you'll have Valencia. After that you'll have a scramble between Athletic Bilbao, Alaves, Espanyol, and Real Betis. And Villarreal might possibly make its way into the mix.

Unless he gets sidelined with an injury, the leading goal-scorer will be Messi.

(1) Real Madrid
(2) Barcelona
(3) Atletico Madrid
(4) Getafe
(5) Sevilla

ITALY
SERIE A

Serie A predictions can be tricky. Will Juventus finally lose some steam? Probably not. In fact, I sincerely doubt it. In first place will be Juventus, followed by Napoli in second, Inter Milan in third, AC Milan in fourth, and Roma—Rome's pride and joy—in fifth. Competitive teams after that will include Atalanta, Torino, Lazio, Sampdoria, and Fiorentina.

The leading scorer in Serie A will be C. Ronaldo.

(1) Juventus
(2) Napoli
(3) Inter Milan
(4) AC Milan
(5) Roma

FRANCE
LIGUE 1

This is how the top 10 in Ligue 1 will finish up in 2019-20, no question:

(1) PSG
(2) LOSC
(3) Saint-Etienne
(4) Lyon
(5) Marseille
(6) Montpellier
(7) Stade de Reims
(8) OGC Nice
(9) Nimes
(10) Strasbourg

As for Bordeaux and Toulouse, it will be very difficult for them to break into the top 10. The same goes for Monaco, Nantes, and Angers. When it comes to PSG, if Neymar remains injury free, it's a team that could soar to first place. If Neymar is injured for a short or extended amount of time, then watch out for LOSC making the league competitive.

Mbappé will likely be the leading scorer in Ligue 1.

2018-19 UEFA CHAMPIONS LEAGUE

The spectacular, coveted, prestigious UEFA Champions League. Clubs of Europe battle it out for continental supremacy, bragging rights, along with a place in history as elite champions for one of the world's most competitive soccer tournaments. Many would argue that the UEFA Champions League is the most prestigious and competitive tournament on earth, even more so than the FIFA World Cup. The reckoning is that club teams spend more time with one another, so therefore the players have a chance to really get into a groove (as opposed to World Cup teams which have less time to practice together). Add to that, Europe attrackts the world's best players, so you have a perfect storm of competition.

Qualifying play took place from June 26 to August 29, 2018. Competition took place from September 18, 2018 to June 1, 2019.

As most everybody knows, during the knockout stage, teams play "two legs" with home and away; overall scores are tallied up. The beauty of this is that if a team doesn't do well in the first leg, it has a chance to redeem itself. Plus, fans get to celebrate a home game.

The championship is one game take all, which is a good idea because there are so many two-leg games leading up to it. It's nice to have suspense with two games, but one game for the final—in a predetermined location—is ideal. One game for the final provides drama. There are no second chances. Everything is riding on that game. It's perfect.

THE UEFA CHAMPIONS LEAGUE GROUPS 2018-19

Group A
Atletico Madrid (w)
Borussia Dortmund (w)
Monaco
Club Brugge

Group B
Barcelona (w)
Inter Milan
Tottenham Hotspur (w)
PSV Eindhoven

Group C
Liverpool (w)
Red Star Belgrade
Napoli
Paris Saint-Germain (w)

Group D
Galatasaray
Porto (w)
Schalke 04 (w)
Lokomotiv Moscow

Group E
Ajax (w)
Bayern Munich (w)
Benfica
AEK Athens

Group F
Lyon (w)
Manchester City (w)
Shakhtar Donetsk
1899 Hoffenheim

Group G
CSKA Moscow
Roma (w)
Real Madrid (w)
Viktoria Plzen

Group H
Juventus (w)
Manchester United (w)
Valencia
Young Boys

Round of 16
(Two legs played)

Schalke 04 vs. Manchester City (w)
Atletico Madrid vs. Juventus (w)
Manchester United (w) vs. Paris Saint-Germain
Tottenham Hotspur (w) vs. Borussia Dortmund

Lyon vs. Barcelona (w)

Roma vs. Porto (w)

Ajax (w) vs. Real Madrid

Liverpool (w) vs. Bayern Munich

ROUND OF 16 HIGHLIGHTS

Real Madrid vs. Ajax

On March 5, 2019, Real Madrid—the mighty giants, the superstars of club soccer—took an embarrassing defeat from Ajax, the ultra-talented Dutch side intent on making a statement. Rory Marsden, writing for *Bleacher Report*, summarized the surreal event: "The superb Dusan Tadic, who set up both first-half goals, then dealt the knockout blow just after the hour, his brilliantly converted strike from the edge of the box eventually being awarded after a lengthy VAR consultation."[56] As a result, Madrid went down hard, dethroned by the energetic Dutch—a side that pressed well and played with swagger.

Tottenham Hotspurs vs. Borussia Dortmund

With a goal from Harry Kane, on March 5, 2019, Tottenham took down the German powerhouse Borussia Dortmund. At the time, Borussia Dortmund was leading the Bundesliga, though Tottenham, playing in a 3-4-1-2, had other ideas.

Quarter-finals

(Two legs played)

Tottenham (w) vs. Manchester City

Liverpool (w) vs. Porto

Ajax (w) vs. Juventus
Manchester United vs. Barcelona (w)

QUARTER-FINALS HIGHLIGHTS

Tottenham vs. Manchester City (Leg 1)
1-0

On April 9, 2019, the first leg of this massive English showdown took place on Tottenham's home turf[3] in front of raucous fans. The bellowing chants signalled the fans were eager for the game to begin. Featured players included Harry Kane and Dele Alli for Tottenham, along with David Silva, Fernandinho, Raheem Sterling, and Sergio Aguero for Manchester City.

Manchester City was awarded an early penalty kick in the first half, which Sergio Aguero missed. Then in the second half, Tottenham rocked the house with a goal by Son Heung-min that would be the decider in the crucial first leg. The game ended 1-0 and a much-anticipated match would arrive in Manchester.

Soccer fans around the world tuned in. In the United States, Steve Nash—the former two-time NBA MVP recipient—joined the party and provided analysis alongside former USMNT players Stuart Holden and Maurice Edu on B/R UEFA Football Matchday and B/R UEFA Football Postmatch which was televised on TNT. (For the American audience, Steve Nash's presence gave soccer—America's fastest growing sport—a lot of street cred; a story for another time.)

---

3 Tottenham Hotspur Stadium.

Liverpool vs. Porto (Leg 1)
2-0

On April 9, 2019, Liverpool tucked away a predictable 2-0 win over Porto in the all-important first leg. Goals were scored by Naby Keita and Firmino as Liverpool got off to a great start.

Ajax vs. Juventus (Leg 1)
1-1

On April 10, 2019, during the first leg, Juventus settled with a tie against talented Ajax. Juventus was on the road and took a 1-0 lead in the first half with a goal from the reliable Ronaldo. Ajax got one back to tie things at 1-1, which was how the game ended. It was glaringly obvious that Ajax was ready for the challenge and Leg 2.

Manchester United vs. Barcelona (Leg 1)
0-1

On April 10, 2019, the result of this first leg was a win for Barcelona in Manchester. A goal from Barcelona came in the first half, and that's how things wound up. Experience led the way for Barca as Manchester United couldn't get a goal on the scoreboard. Featured players included Messi, Coutinho, Suarez, and Pique for Barcelona, along with Pogba, Rashford, and Fred for Manchester United. It was a missed opportunity at home for Manchester, considering the second leg would be played at Camp Nou where Messi and company typically have a strong advantage.

Tottenham vs. Manchester City (Leg 2)
3-4

On April 17, 2019, the big showdown took place in Manchester. For Tottenham, star forward Harry Kane was out with an injury. Dele Alli had to pick up the slack. Manchester City had Kevin De Bruyne and David Silva in the starting lineup. Despite being the favorite, Manchester City needed a break; it needed to get out in front. Raheem Sterling stepped up and did just that, scoring a goal early in the first half to put City on top.

Shortly after, Tottenham leveled things out at 1-1. Son Heung-min got the goal. Then, if you can believe it, shortly after that Son Heung-min scored again! (Given the aggregate score, Manchester City needed to score four goals to have a chance.) Amazingly, a short time later, City scored again. Back and forth, back and forth. The play was incredible. It was level, 2-2. And it was only the beginning portion of the first half!

Who could've guessed it? It was assumed that Manchester City—the powerhouse passing squad that it was—was going to idle the game away, albeit with exciting flurries here and there, and take away the clock for a predictable win at home. Instead, a dramatic four goals lit up the stadium.

It wasn't over. Manchester City got a third, making it 3-2. Yes, still in the first half! It was stated on the B/R UEFA Football Matchday halftime show as being the fastest five goals in Champions League history.

As the second half progressed it happened: Manchester City surged forward, and Sergio Aguero put one in, making it 4-2. Just when things were going well for City, Tottenham got one back. VAR was consulted, and the goal was allowed. The score was 4-3.

It still wasn't over. At the close of the game Raheem Sterling seemingly put City into the semi-finals with his goal... but it was offside.

With that the game ended 4-3, in favor of City. However, overall, from the first and second legs, the aggregate score ended 4-4, and based on away goals, Tottenham advanced to the semi-finals.

Pep Guardiola—with all his coaching brilliance—couldn't pull it off. Would he stay on as coach? Would this be the beginning of the end for Pep in Manchester City? It wouldn't be out of the question for Guardiola to move on and seek Champions League glory at another powerhouse club. Or he might stay on board with City and see what can be done about another run at the Champions League. (This would be speculation for another day. Manchester City had to finish up Premier League play as it was chasing Liverpool on route to a possible first-place finish.) The end result on this date was as brilliant game, a letdown for Manchester City, and a huge relief for Tottenham fans.

Liverpool vs. Porto (Leg 2)
4-1

On April 17, 2019, Mo Salah and the highly favored Liverpool confidently took the field in the second leg against Porto, a worthy opponent but not one expected to get past this round. Liverpool got out to a 1-0 lead in the first half. The final result of the second leg was a 4-1 win for Liverpool, and it advanced to the semi-finals.

Ajax vs. Juventus (Leg 2)
2-1

On April 16, 2019, during the second leg, Ronaldo and Juventus had a challenge in the form of Ajax, a Dutch club ready for any opponent. The first half ended 1-1. The second half proved to be in favor of the Dutch. Juventus—the Serie A giants—fell to Ajax by a score of 2-1. Juventus had acquired Ronaldo in hopes of gaining the illustrious Champions League trophy. Ajax—with the help of Donny van de Beek and Matthijs de Ligt—had other plans and moved on to the semi-finals.

Manchester United vs. Barcelona (Leg 2)
3-0

On April 16, 2019, Manchester United made the relatively short trip to Barcelona for the second leg at the renowned and feared Camp Nou. Things didn't start out very well for the English visitors, to say the least. Messi got on the scoreboard with two in the first half. The stadium boomed in excitement. The first half ended 2-0 for Barca. As for the second half, Barca continued with a goal from Coutinho. Manchester United was devastated as Barcelona pocketed a huge victory at home, earning a place in the semi-finals.

Semi-finals
(Two legs played)

Tottenham (w) vs. Ajax
Barcelona vs. Liverpool (w)

SEMI-FINALS HIGHLIGHTS

Tottenham vs. Ajax (Leg 1)
1-0

Finally, on April 30, 2019, the semi-finals rolled around. The first half started out well for Ajax. Donny van de Beek got the first goal. Ajax looked good on the road. That was how it ended. Ajax outplayed Tottenham, with better technique and passing. Tottenham gave it a go, but it wasn't enough. The first leg, the all-important first leg, went to the Dutch.

Barcelona vs. Liverpool (Leg 1)
3-0

Of the two semi-finals, this was the big one. The proverbial heavyweights. As much as Ajax and Tottenham brought quality to the other semi-final, the showdown on May 1, 2019, between Barcelona and Liverpool, both number one in their respective leagues at the time, was going to be extra special. After all, as the game kicked off, Liverpool featured Mo Salah, who was top of the scoring list in England (with 21), though, it's fair to say, he had a little competition from a few others, hungry goal-scorers eager to take the lead, including Sadio Mane (his Liverpool teammate) and Sergio Aguero (of Manchester City). Meanwhile, on the other side, Barcelona had someone named Messi, who was far out in front as the leading scorer in Spain (with 34). His Barcelona teammate, Luis Suarez, was top of the list as well. But scoring titles aside, the game was on. In fact, the ubiquitous goal-scoring threat Suarez was the first on the board, getting one against his old team with a goal in the first half that put Barca ahead at home by a score of 1-0.

As the second half lingered on, Messi—the world's greatest player—stepped up big time and got two goals, making it 3-0. Mo Salah—who, alongside fellow soccer player, Alex Morgan, was part of *Time Magazine's* 100 Most Influential People list of 2019—was relatively quiet, with a few moments here and there. All in all, he didn't give quite the performance he had hoped he would. The overwhelming fortress of Camp Nou—including the chants and drum beats from a throng the size of a large city—proved too much for Liverpool.

Liverpool vs. Barcelona (Leg 2)
4-0

Liverpool hosted the second leg bout on May 7, 2019. Liverpoolsuffered a 3-0 loss in the first leg and had to overcome a big deficit at home. It wouldn't have Mo Salah. Fabinho would need to step up big-time. It would be up to Barcelona—with Messi, Suarez, and Vidal—to win to ensure its place in the final. In the first half, Liverpool got off to a great start by asserting a 1-0 lead.

Then in the second half, in quick succession, Liverpool got two goals, making it 3-0, and the crowd went wild. There was so much emotion in the stadium. Liverpool was back. Then a fourth came. It was astounding. Liverpool acquired a 4-0 lead in a game that needed just that. At last, the final whistle blew, and the Liverpool faithful went mad with a thunderous roar. Anfield was rocking. It was curtains for Barcelona. What a performance for Liverpool. The home of The Beatles was soaring with excitement. Who would've thought? Sure, Liverpool is a top-notch heavyweight club, but Barcelona? The masters of possession, the masters of closing games out. Liverpool faced a challenge and it rose to that challenge, pulling off a magnificent 4-0 victory—4-3 on aggregate—which secured a place in the Champions League final for the second year in a row. Anfield holds around 54,000, and the chanting and singing lingered in the air, like a grand, megachurch experience in the world of soccer.

Tottenham vs. Ajax (Leg 2)
3-2

The last semi-final took place on May 8, 2019. Ajax was ready to go. This was it. It had one game to reintroduce itself to the Champions League championship match, a place it had been numerous times before. Tottenham, after enduring a first-leg loss at home, was up against them.

Ajax hosted and hit the first half rolling with two goals, the first of which came from Matthijs de Ligt, the young 19-year-old captain. The first half for Tottenham—not good. Tottenham didn't have an answer. It ended 2-0 in favor of Ajax.

As for the second half, which represented Tottenham's last chance to make a stand, things got interesting. The Spurs got on the board with two goals, equalizing the game at 2-2. The Tottenham fans went wild. The game was all tied up. Then, if you can believe it, Lucas Moura, Tottenham's last hope it would seem, got the third goal right at the close of the match. On top of that, it was a hat-trick for Moura. It was epic, dramatic, and unbelievable. Without the presence of Harry Kane, Tottenham found a way to the championship game in Madrid. It would be Tottenham versus Liverpool, an all-England final.

These semi-final matches wrapped up an amazing year for European club soccer and the Champions League. It was a breathtaking finale, one that captivated fans around the globe.

FINAL

Liverpool vs. Tottenham
2-0

Champions: Liverpool

Led by Mo Salah and German coach, Jürgen Klopp, Liverpool reached the mountaintop of European soccer, yet again.

For many people, the quarter-finals and semi-finals are the greatest parts of a tournament. In fact, the reasoning behind this type of thinking is that the final is kind of sad because it's the last game. Then it's all over. But with the quarter- and semi-finals, there's always another game down the road. For the 2018-19 Champions League it was no different. There was excitement and drama surrounding the much-anticipated quarters and semis, and the eventual 2018-19 champions made out with a treasured trophy that was highly deserved. The 2018-19 year marked another brilliant Champions League chapter in soccer history, and that of the world. It's why fans get ready for the tournament to start up all over again the following year.

The name has changed over the years. Previously, it was called the European Cup. Now, obviously, it is UEFA Champions League. The following is the list of European club champions prior to 2018-19:

1955-56	Real Madrid	1959-60	Real Madrid
1956-57	Real Madrid	1960-61	Benfica
1957-58	Real Madrid	1961-62	Benfica
1958-59	Real Madrid	1962-63	AC Milan

1963-64	Inter Milan	1991-92	Barcelona
1964-65	Inter Milan	1992-93	Marseille
1965-66	Real Madrid	1993-94	AC Milan
1966-67	Celtic	1994-95	Ajax
1967-68	Manchester United	1995-96	Juventus
1968-69	AC Milan	1996-97	Borussia Dortmund
1969-70	Feyenoord	1997-98	Real Madrid
1970-71	Ajax	1998-99	Manchester United
1971-72	Ajax	1999-00	Real Madrid
1972-73	Ajax	2000-01	Bayern Munich
1973-74	Bayern Munich	2001-02	Real Madrid
1974-75	Bayern Munich	2002-03	AC Milan
1975-76	Bayern Munich	2003-04	Porto
1976-77	Liverpool	2004-05	Liverpool
1977-78	Liverpool	2005-06	Barcelona
1978-79	Nottingham Forest	2006-07	AC Milan
1979-80	Nottingham Forest	2007-08	Manchester United
1980-81	Liverpool	2008-09	Barcelona
1981-82	Aston Villa	2009-10	Inter Milan
1982-83	Hamburg	2010-11	Barcelona
1983-84	Liverpool	2011-12	Chelsea
1984-85	Juventus	2012-13	Bayern Munich
1985-86	Steaua Bucuresti	2013-14	Real Madrid
1986-87	Porto	2014-15	Barcelona
1987-88	PSV Eindhoven	2015-16	Real Madrid
1988-89	AC Milan	2016-17	Real Madrid
1989-90	AC Milan	2017-18	Real Madrid
1990-91	Red Star Belgrade	2018-19	Liverpool

2019-20 UEFA CHAMPIONS LEAGUE: A LOOK AHEAD

Without a doubt, the leaders going into the 2019-20 Champions League tournament are Barcelona, Ajax, Tottenham, Real Madrid, Bayern Munich, Juventus, Manchester City, and Paris Saint-Germain. Will other teams sneak in and make a strong move? Sure, it's possible. AC Milan, Porto, and Benfica certainly will have something to say about it. Watch for Real Madrid under its new (and former) coach, Zinedine Zidane.

BEST OF THE REST—THE TOP 5 TEAMS FROM OTHER COUNTRIES

AJAX

Twitter: @AFCAjax
Founded in 1900
Netherlands Football League Championship (Eredivisie): 33
KNVB Cup: 18
Johan Cruyff Shield (Dutch Super Cup): 8
European Cup and UEFA Champions League: 4
UEFA Super Cup: 2

Known For
Very passionate fans
Exciting games
A strong program
Johan Cruyff
Frank Rijkaard
Ronald Koeman
Marco van Basten
Dennis Bergkamp
Marc Overmars
Frank de Boer
Ronald de Boer

Jan Vertonghen
Luis Suarez
Donny van de Beek
Matthijs de Ligt

A BRIEF TEAM HISTORY

By the time this book was published, Ajax—also known as AFC Ajax—had acquired 33 Eredivisie titles (which, you guessed it, is a lot), 18 KNVB Cups (yes, that's a lot, too), and 8 Johan Cruyff Shields. To say that Ajax's streak is over would be insane. It's one of the most elite Dutch clubs in the country's history, and it has proven to be a success wherever it has competed.

As for the UEFA Champions League, Ajax has gained four titles to date (1970-71, 1971-72, 1972-73, and 1994-95), and each year it's looking like a potential contender; nothing is off the table for Ajax.

Throughout its long, prominent history, Ajax has featured many of the world's greatest players. Some of those include Johan Cruyff, Frank Rijkaard, Ronald Koeman, Marco van Basten, Dennis Bergkamp, Marc Overmars, Frank de Boer, Ronald de Boer, and Luis Suarez.

The success of Ajax continues to this day. For a club that is renowned for its detailed approach to short passing (a world leader, in fact), things are only looking up for the Dutch masters.

FACTS ABOUT THEIR CITY

Amsterdam is lined with dikes, which are embankments that were built to prevent flooding from the sea. Amsterdam has long been a seaport city, a launching point to the rest of the world. Overseas trade and the intermingling of different cultures have been a prevalent in Amsterdam for hundreds of years. It's been known for shipbuilding, dairy products, and beer. When it comes to beer, the Netherlands at large has become associated with Heineken beer. In 1864, Gerard Adriaan Heineken convinced his wealthy mother to buy The Haystack (De Hooiberg in Dutch) brewery in Amsterdam. It had been brewing a popular working-class beer since 1592. In 1873, after hiring a a student of Louis Pasteur, Dr. Elion, to develop Heineken, the HBM (Heineken's Bierbrouwerij Maatschappij) was established, and the first Heineken brand beer was brewed."[57]

Ajax, the passing wonders, play out of Amsterdam. Johan Cruyff Arena—its stadium—holds around 54,000 people. It became available for use in 1996. As a club, Ajax has been known to house numerous youth programs, all of which train under the same system of play, adding value to the senior team.

WHERE THE TEAM IS TODAY— TACTICS AND STRATEGIES

In 2018-19, Ajax was seen using a 4-2-3-1 or a 4-3-3. It's a club that excels in the areas of short passing, combination passing, overlapping runs, and exploiting open space. It's all there. Superb passing came from numerous players, notably Donny van de Beek, Dušan Tadić, and Matthijs de Ligt.

Tactics and strategies: keep the team together.

Ajax is often used as a steppingstone by players, and it's seen as such by larger, better regarded clubs. Even still, Ajax is about as well-regarded as any club. However, many top clubs around the world will raid a place like Ajax for up-and-coming talent, so really it would be in Ajax's best interest to somehow hold on to its young stars. It will be difficult because big offers are alluring. However, if Ajax can keep its current nucleus together, it has a lot of potential to achieve fantastic things in the next five to eight years.

ERIK TEN HAG—A BRIEF COACHING PORTRAIT

Erik ten Hag—who was born in 1970—played as a central defender with Twente and Utrecht. Prior to taking on the job with Ajax, he coached at Utrecht. Now in firm control of one of the Netherlands top clubs, Erik ten Hag is at the forefront of global soccer as his side made a tremendous run in the 2018-19 Champions League. It also flourished at the top of the charts in the Eredivisie. With coach Erik ten Hag, expect to see a 4-2-3-1 or a 4-3-3. Odds are, it'll be a 4-3-3, which, to be honest, is the better of the two; it allows for more pressure to be applied on the defensive side, and the passing combinations can be more effective—over time—on the offensive side of the ball. All and all, his team provided a lot of excitement last season and was a joy to watch as it exhibited great passing, exciting runs, and confident play. Without a doubt, credit should go to coach Erik ten Hag for gearing up a very young team to perform so competently on such a big stage. That's not always the easiest thing to do, even with a club like Ajax that has an extensive youth academy system that trains its players for the big games, yet he pulled it off and deserves a lot of credit for it.

KEY PLAYERS AND THEIR CHARACTERISTICS

Donny van de Beek, Dušan Tadić, and Matthijs de Ligt

The vibrant, structured, organized, and free-wheeling Dutch side Ajax is led, in part, by **Donny van de Beek**. He was born in 1997 in the Netherlands. In terms of the Champions League competition, he was one of the young players that led Ajax to such great heights. He brings a high level of skill, touch, and knowledge to the game. Much more is expected of him throughout a highly anticipated career, one that is just starting.

Dušan Tadić—who is a veteran with Serbia's national team— is an attacking midfielder who arrived in Ajax after a stop in the Premier League playing for Southampton. He'll typically be found up top causing havoc, and he's scored over 20 goals with Ajax so far. He arrived in 2018, and it seems like there's much more around the corner for the talented Tadić.

Believe it or not, **Matthijs de Ligt**—who was only born in 1999—has already become captain of Ajax. He came up through the club's youth system. With Ajax's senior team, the extremely young defender has already gained over 70 appearances. His composure and confidence at such a young age will prove overwhelming for opponents. Matthijs de Ligt is slowly gaining ground as a household name, and whether he reaches the level of a Franz Beckenbauer or Franco Baresi or Ronald Koeman is unknown, yet he's off to a good start (considering, for example, his amazing run in the 2018-19 UEFA Champions League). His time with Ajax and that of the Dutch national team will be a telling indicator of how far he can get.

Overall Player Rating:
Donny van de Beek: 9.3
Dušan Tadić: 9.3
Matthijs de Ligt: 9.5

KEY PLAYER STATS

(Total career goals with this club)

	Games Played	Goals
Donny van de Beek	91	19
Dušan Tadić	32	24
Matthijs de Ligt	75	8

WHAT TO WATCH FOR ON TV—HOW MESSI, NEYMAR, RONALDO, AND OTHERS PLAY

Traditionally, Ajax has been a roadmap for coaches to rely on, that's for sure, and, not to mention, Ajax has provided a platform for coaches to acquire top-level talent. Generation after generation, Ajax has produced players that know how to pass the ball within a system of play that stresses quick and smart combination passing. It sounds so easy, like something that any coach or player outside of Ajax could achieve, yet it's more difficult than people think. It's why places like Jamaica, Tunisia, Paraguay, and the United States haven't won the World Cup. Neither has the Netherlands, but it's always been regarded as one of the two best soccer-playing countries to never win the World Cup (the other was Spain, prior to its first title in 2010). Before you wonder why we've transitioned to talking about national teams, you have to remember that the approach of club and national teams is often intertwined, if not completely one hundred percent intertwined. As it turns out, whether we're talking about youth, professional, or national team levels, Ajax has been an ideal for how teams strive to play.

Coaches yearn for practically anything Ajax has to offer. Getting a group of guys onto the same page—within a systematic approach to passing a simple round ball—is something that has kept coaches up at night for over a hundred years. Yet Ajax—which essentially has been a torchbearer for Dutch soccer alongside the Dutch national team—has ostensibly found the magic formula. It practically invented it. This is why club and national team coaches have sought tips from the Dutch masters. After all, the former Ajax superstar and legend Johan Cruyff brought this magical Dutch touch to Barcelona, and since then La Masia has produced brilliant players for Barca's first team which has trickled over to the national team, and, as many believe (rightly so), this was the cause for all the success that the Golden Generation had, including Spain's first World Cup trophy in South Africa.

When analyzing the "Ajax approach" (or the "Dutch approach"), some stress triangle passing combinations, while others focus on more of the inherent connection between the players on the field (whether they're combining passes in a triangular shape or not). However one quantifies Ajax's approach, the end result has been brilliant, crisp, and eye-pleasing play whenever an Ajax team sets foot on a pitch. That's the bottom line. On top of that, Ajax develops skillful players at each position. The overall effect is that wherever you look there are technically sound players that are perspicacious to any situation on the field. This 2019-20 campaign will be no different. The players are top class; the coaching is top class. However, given its extreme success in 2018-19, Ajax might lose a few players due to trades. But this shouldn't suggest that Ajax is reliant on star players. Star players? Who needs star players when you're Ajax? If Ajax loses a player, the next one up will be quality. It has a strong bullpen, with strength in its academy system, so Ajax will remain a top club in the Netherlands, and don't be surprised to see another impressive push toward the UEFA Champions League trophy.

WHAT ARE THEIR CHANCES OF WINNING THE LEAGUE TITLE THIS YEAR?

Extremely good. It will be either Ajax or PSV.

Overall Team Ranking: 9.5-9.7

BENFICA

Twitter: @slbenfica_en
Founded in 1904
Primeira Liga Titles: 36
Taça de Portugal: 26
European Cup and UEFA Champions League: 2
UEFA Super Cup: 0

Known For
The early 1960s
Very passionate fans
Exciting games
Eusebio
João Félix
Rúben Dias
Haris Seferović

A BRIEF TEAM HISTORY

Essentially Benfica has more or less dominated the Primeira Liga with 36 titles to date (a crazy amount), and many more to come. The early 1960s were great years for Benfica as it won the European Cup on two occasions in 1960-61 and 1961-62. This was the Eusebio era. Eusebio—who played for Benfica from 1961-75—is arguably the best player to have walked through the club's doors. As a Portuguese national team standout, Eusebio is in the running, along with Cristiano Ronaldo, for the best Portuguese player of all time. He left an impressive signature with the club, scoring 317 goals in 301 appearances. Then he tumbled into a string of different contracts, ending with the Buffalo Stallions of the Major Indoor Soccer League (MISL). He'll be remembered most, though, for his time with Benfica during a beautiful era of soccer—the 1960s—in which Pele, Garrincha, and George Best were flying high. This era was the last time to date that Benfica has won the highest prize in European club soccer.

FACTS ABOUT THEIR CITY

Benfica sits on a Portuguese soccer throne in Lisbon, Portugal's capital. It's a city with a population of around 500,000. Portugal, which often might be overlooked as a place to visit, has an alluring vibe about it. Much of the partying in Portugal has to do with soccer, the country's pastime. Estádio da Luz would be the stadium that fans flock to. It holds around 64,000. As stadiums go, it's pretty new as it became available for use back in 2003. Come game time, when Benfica takes the field, many fans might be guzzling Sagres beer or Super Bock, popular brews from Portugal.

WHERE THE TEAM IS TODAY—
TACTICS AND STRATEGIES

Benfica used the 4-2-3-1 or a 4-4-2 to its optimum advantage as it dominated the Primeira Liga.

Tactics and strategies: get the most out of João Félix and Haris Seferović.

There are plenty of players to help along the way, such as Ljubomir Fejsa, Rúben Dias, Pizzi, Andreas Samaris, and center mid Florentino Luís. Perhaps the best way to elevate the salient talent on the team is to first improve its overall approach to possession. This will open up many more opportunities for João Félix and Haris Seferović, who have the skill to put away a ton of goals.

This is a very good team, a talented group, a club with many weapons. Now, it fell short recently in its attempt at Champions League glory, but it's definitely a strong presence in Portugal with a lot to prove on the continent. As to whether it can achieve the highest success again is another question. Can it? Yes. Will it? No, probably not any time soon unless it grooms a special generation of young players and then holds on to those young players. But as far as special generations go, it would have to be a group that is in sync with possession-oriented passing, similar to Barcelona and its approach. Anything else probably won't work for Benfica. But let's not get carried away. Its first challenge is to find a special generation of young players. Then, it needs to toughen up its attitude for the big dogs in Europe (Real Madrid, Bayern Munich, etc.). Though if it neglects a firm approach to possession and decides to exchange punches with other teams, it will only be disappointing itself and its fans on a run for

Champions League glory. However, if it consolidates its efforts into a rhythmic and cohesive possession-oriented approach to the game, then, outside of Portugal, it has a chance to shake things up like in the early 60s.

BRUNO LAGE—A BRIEF COACHING PORTRAIT

Bruno Lage—who was born in 1976 in Portugal—has held several coaching positions—including recent stops as an assistant with Sheffield Wednesday and Swansea City—until landing the head coaching position with Benfica in 2019. Sitting atop Portuguese soccer, he has many talented players to act out his vision—which has taken the form of a 4-2-3-1 and 4-4-2—including Ljubomir Fejsa, Rúben Dias, Haris Seferović, Pizzi, Andreas Samaris, Florentino Luís, and João Félix. While Lage might be sitting in a comfortable position domestically, his hopes of making an impression in UEFA Champions League competition may be an audacious aspiration.

KEY PLAYERS AND THEIR CHARACTERISTICS

João Félix, Rúben Dias, and Haris Seferović

João Félix is a young player who was born in 1999 in Portugal. With his exceptional dribbling skills, the dynamic midfielder has proven to be a handful at the top Portuguese level. He has a knack for getting around defenders, and this sets him apart as a sought-after, up-and-coming talent. How long will Félix stay with

Benfica? This is a good question, and don't be surprised to see him traded, possibly to an elite club like Liverpool, Real Madrid, or AC Milan, sometime soon.

Rúben Dias is another young player on the squad. Dias was born in 1997, and the central defender already has a handful of games with Portugal under his belt. As a steady presence on defense, he also has the ability to put in a few goals along the way.

Haris Seferović—a forward with Switzerland—has a point to make with his play. He joined Benfica in 2017 and has flourished, scoring more than 20 goals. He was brought in to produce, and he's done just that. How much more can he offer? Fans of Benfica are hoping for a lot more, and the pressure is on Seferović to stay consistent. Otherwise, he might be on a train back to Grasshopper Club Zurich, where he started his career.

Overall Player Rating:
João Félix: 9.2
Rúben Dias: 8.8
Haris Seferović: 8.9

KEY PLAYER STATS

(Total career goals with this club)

	Games Played	Goals
João Félix	22	13
Rúben Dias	48	5
Haris Seferović	44	23

WHAT TO WATCH FOR ON TV—HOW MESSI, NEYMAR, RONALDO, AND OTHERS PLAY

Benfica will exploit the wings and use its speed to take advantage of weaknesses in its opponent's defense. This, coupled with skillful midfield play, is a strong combination which has set Benfica apart from rival Portuguese clubs.

One area of concern, an area that could be improved upon, would be one-on-one defensive lapses from time to time. Is this enough to halt a team in its tracks? Oddly enough, it can be. Little things like one-on-one defense and tight marking can differentiate good players from great ones, and this affects to programs on a whole, which explains why recently Barcelona and Real Madrid have had much better chances to excel in the Champions League than a team like Benfica.

Typically, Manchester United's program has found players that are excellent at one-on-one situations. Anderson—the defensive midfielder from Brazil—is a great example of the type of player that set United apart from lesser teams. During his time with the club, most, if not all, one-on-one tackles and one-on-one battles went in favor of United. During Anderson's time with United (2007-2015), especially in the first few years, the club was about as good as a team can get. Anderson was feisty, feistier than most, but each United player on the field had similar one-on-one defensive qualities; it was a team that had few slip-ups on defense and most tackles went its way.

If possible, Benfica needs to hone in on such a thing. The talent is there. The history is there. Benfica needs to consolidate its collective resources, with experienced coaching, training methods, and recruiting, to better itself—to step into the forefront of Europe as a true bellwether. It needs to repudiate "a little better than average" and live up to the standards set by Bayern Munich, Liverpool, Manchester City, Barcelona, and Real Madrid. After all, hoping for a savior like Eusebio to show up in the eleventh hour and turn all of Benfica's *maybes* and *what ifs* into a return to the promise land might be asking a lot.

Such a team exists, and it's a matter of Benfica recognizing it. Until it finally reaches that first-place podium, it will remain a fascinating club that constantly teases its fans with the hopes and dreams of returning to its former glory.

WHAT ARE THEIR CHANCES OF WINNING THE LEAGUE TITLE THIS YEAR?

Very good. If not for Porto, Benfica would likely be sitting pretty in first place.

Overall Team Ranking: 8.9

PORTO

Twitter: @FCPorto
Founded in 1893
Primeira Liga Titles: 28
Taça de Portugal: 16
European Cup and UEFA Champions League: 2
UEFA Super Cup: 1

Known For
Strong attendance
Very passionate fans
Exciting games
Bobby Robson
Rabah Madjer
Pepe
Héctor Herrera
Jesús Corona
Danilo Pereira

A BRIEF TEAM HISTORY

FC Porto was founded in 1893. Take that, AC Milan. Porto, to say the least, has a bit of history. It has owned the Primeira Liga on plenty of occasions, taking 28 titles. As for the Taça de Portugal, it's done very well, earning 16 titles. Porto's success hasn't just been relegated to Portugal. It won the European Cup (later renamed to UEFA Champions League) in 1986-87 and 2003-04. It also won the UEFA Super Cup in 1987. During 2018-19, Porto did well in the Champions League, but not well enough. It found a place in the quarter-finals only to lose out to Liverpool in two legs.

FACTS ABOUT THEIR CITY

Porto—which sits in the north of Portugal overlooking the Atlantic Ocean—has a population of around 287,000 people. Near Porto is a popular wine-making region known as the Douro Valley, a place that tourists from around the world visit, taking in an assortment of wines while experiencing the beautiful scenic area firsthand. Intertwined in the culture of Portugal, and that of Porto, would be soccer. For each game, thousands of Porto fans make their way to Estádio do Dragão, the home stadium that holds approximately 50,000. It's a rowdy place that embraces the hopes and dreams of fans eager to capture another Champions League title.

WHERE THE TEAM IS TODAY—TACTICS AND STRATEGIES

In 2018-19, Porto typically went with a 4-4-2 (a trusty formation). Against Liverpool in the Champions League, Porto opted for a 3-4-3 and a 4-2-2-2. During 2018-19 a few featured players were Yacine Brahimi, Moussa Marega, Héctor Herrera, Danilo Pereira, Jesús Corona, and forwardsMoussa Marega of Mali, Yacine Brahimi (a big scorer), Otávio, and Tiquinho—who also goes by Francisco Soaresand is a scoring threat. Pepe—who spent a long time with Real Madrid—is an experienced defender who will continue adding strength and stability on the back line. Next to him will be Felipe, a Brazilian center defender. The two should be a great combination for Porto to build on. Unless some last-minute trades occur, much of this roster should remain the same. On top of its experienced defense, Porto has a vibrant attack that can electrify the wings. Likely, considering its impressive lineup, Porto will win the Primeira Liga in 2019-20 and make a strong run at the Champions League.

Tactics and strategies: keep the flow of play going through Héctor Herrera and try to build around him.

Herrera is super talented, and if the team can add a few strong pieces around him, things should get even better.

SÉRGIO CONCEIÇÃO—A BRIEF COACHING PORTRAIT

The man leading the show in Porto is coach Sérgio Conceição, a former Porto player. He was also a member of Portugal's national team. Conceição—who was born in 1974—brings a wealth of playing experience to the table, and he favors the 4-4-2, which was evident in 2018-19. Leading the fight in Porto is an exciting development under Conceição. He has an assortment of talent, ranging from Héctor Herrera to Jesús Corona to Danilo Pereira, and the list goes on. It should be an exciting year for Porto, and while the Primeira Liga may be in hand, the question of Champions League glory is yet to be determined as Conceição will be applying his tactical thoughts to the task of winning European club soccer's biggest prize.

KEY PLAYERS AND THEIR CHARACTERISTICS

Héctor Herrera, Jesús Corona, and Danilo Pereira

With a little scrutiny, you can see that Mexican international **Héctor Herrera** is a special center midfielder with smarts, skill, and touch. In *THE World Cup 2018 Book: Everything You Need to Know About the Soccer World Cup*, he was ranked number 10 out of all players in the tournament. Without a doubt, in the past few years, he's made a name for himself as arguably the best center mid in CONCACAF. But what he does is usually nuanced and hard to detect at first glance. Is he fast? No, not at all. Is he quick? Not really. Is he a dangerous dribbler? Not so much. He's crafty, but nothing to write home about. Is he a goal-scoring threat? Not exactly.[4] So why bother with this guy? What's his deal? He has a high soccer IQ. More than anything

---

4 He does have over 20 goals for Porto, but it's not the first thing that comes to mind.

else, his strength rests in his ability to guide the game with an organizational touch (including tiny chips, balls played with a little bit of english and side spin when necessary), and, in doing so, he sets up his teammates left and right with arranged passes—indeed, *high quality* passes—all over the field.

Jesús Corona was a great score for Porto. The Mexican international winger, who is now in his mid-twenties, is a sensational talent out wide, one that adds a special dimension to the lineup. Is he fast? Yes. Is he quick? Yes. Can he dribble? Yes. Most important, when it comes to dribbling, does he have an innate will to get around defenders? Yes, and often they're befuddled as he rumbles by.

Certainly Moussa Marega, Tiquinho, and Yacine Brahimi could have been featured in this Key Players section; however, **Danilo Pereira**, the center midfielder alongside Herrera, has been instrumental in getting the ball distributed around the field thus setting up the aforementioned players. Pereira—who was born in 1991 and plays on Portugal's national team—brings trust to the midfield, a consistency, that helps others score goals, and that's an important trait to have.

Overall Player Rating:
Héctor Herrera: 9.5
Jesús Corona: 9.6
Danilo Pereira: 8.9

KEY PLAYER STATS

(Total career goals with this club)

	Games Played	Goals
Héctor Herrera	161	25
Jesús Corona	108	15
Danilo Pereira	100	12

WHAT TO WATCH FOR ON TV—HOW MESSI, NEYMAR, RONALDO, AND OTHERS PLAY

There is talent, along with smart players, on Porto. A lot of scoring opportunities should come from Moussa Marega, Tiquinho, and Yacine Brahimi. It's a team that could really get going after turning on the turbo jets. It met its match last season against Liverpool in the Champions League, but it can build on that progress for another run, and the sky's the limit. As for league play, expect to see exciting games rich with goals from a seemingly unstoppable Porto side. The only thing stopping it might be Benfica (Porto's *bête noire* of the highest order), but aside from that Porto is gearing up for a great 2019-20 season.

With the recent acquisition of Pepe—who, yes, is getting older in soccer years—Porto has a solid performer who will add stability to Porto's defense, and this is essential for a club—with so much talent—to move forward. Despite his age, Porto fans should be excited about Pepe's presence; as a result, the next few years could be very interesting for the club. Felipe also adds a strong presence on defense, which will be an important aspect of Porto's long-term success. It's a balanced team fulldeep of international talent that is bound to bring excitement to each game.

WHAT ARE THEIR CHANCES OF WINNING THE LEAGUE TITLE THIS YEAR?

Extremely high. Porto and Benfica will be leading the way.

Overall Team Ranking: 9.1

CELTIC

Twitter: @CelticFC
Founded in 1887
League Championship: 50
Scottish Cup: 38
Scottish League Cup: 18
European Cup and UEFA Champions League: 1
UEFA Super Cup: 0

Known For
Strong attendance
Very passionate fans
Exciting games
Billy McNeill
Jimmy Johnstone
Kenny Dalglish
Callum McGregor
Scott Brown
James Forrest
Nir Bitton

A BRIEF TEAM HISTORY

The green and white stripes of Celtic F.C. linger in the hearts and minds of fans that have lived with the team for a lifetime. The roots of fandom for Celtic run deep. Since 1887, when the club was introduced, generations have passed, and the anthem for Celtic marches forward.

Basically, it's fair to say that Celtic has kept trophy manufacturers and trophy-case manufacturers in business for a long time. In the lexicon of its storied existence in the Scottish Premiership, Celtic has represented quality. It has won the league championship an astounding 49 times as of the 2017-18 season. The season of 2018-19 made it an even 50, for now. Certainly 54 titles are right around the corner, and 72 will be soon after that. But, what has been even more amazing, was that Celtic has been on a roll of late—similar to Juventus—with consecutive league championships from 2011-12, 2012-13, 2013-14, 2014-15, 2015-16, 2016-17, 2017-18, and 2018-19. Celtic won the European Cup (later renamed UEFA Champions League) in 1966-67. Perhaps soon, given its strong run in Scotland, Celtic will be back on top of Europe's finest club tournament.

Getting there might prove tricky given a recent shift in the coaching department. In 2019, upon hearing the news of coach Brendan Rodgers leaving the club, even Rod Stewart had something to say. As *CNN* reported, "A huge Celtic fan, who is often pictured watching the team play at Celtic Park, Stewart said the news had 'ruined my holiday' after hearing Rodgers was ready to leave the Scottish champion and instead move back to the English Premier League with Leicester City. After arriving at Celtic in 2016, Rodgers won every single domestic trophy he's competed in, including two league titles, three League Cups and two Scottish Cups. But on Tuesday, he signed a deal until 2022 with Leicester, leaving Celtic midway through its pursuit of a domestic Treble—a feat it has achieved in each of the previous two seasons."[58]

It's a club that has been setting the way in Scotland, and, even with a new direction and manager, it should continue to flourish domestically. The next two to five years will be telling.

FACTS ABOUT THEIR CITY

Celtic Park, a legendary stadium with history dating back to 1892, holds a little over 60,000 strong. It's a gem of Glasgow, Scotland, home of Celtic. If there's a game, you'll know it; the chanting starts, and a briskly paced race up and down the field begins. When a home-goal is scored, the fans erupt into thunderous celebration. It's what they live for. Celtic brings so much pride to the city and its people. It's clearly the number one show in town. The beer flows, and the celebratory ritual of Celtic games carries on, as it did 54 years ago and as it will continue to do so into the next century.

WHERE THE TEAM IS TODAY— TACTICS AND STRATEGIES

Watch for a 4-4-2 or possibly a 4-2-3-1. Both formations were used in the 2018-19 season, and this playing style will likely remain the same. This is particularly true based on Celtic's outstanding success in the Scottish Premiership. It's *the* team right now.

Tactics and strategies: keep the momentum going and stay consistent.

There isn't much Celtic is doing wrong in Scotland at the moment. If it continues on the same path, it will likely win the league championship this year and the following one as well. As for progress in the Champions League, Celtic might have a different challenge. Within Scotland, Celtic's approach is clearly working. Outside of that it's a competitive club, there's no questioning that, but there's something missing. It can't keep up with Barcelona or Real Madrid, for example, two clubs that excel at possession-oriented soccer in the modern era. Celtic likes to push the pace and trade punches. Does it use possession? Sure. But not like Barcelona, Real Madrid, Ajax, or Bayern Munich. If Celtic moves toward more of a possession-oriented approach (one that might resemble tiki-taka), is it fair to say that it would be abandoning what already works so well? Yes, possibly. It might backfire and cause the team to crumble in confidence. When a side is used to getting at it, and pushing the pace with opponents, any change in style might be very counterproductive. For now, Celtic is achieving brilliant results in Scotland, but it might want to consider a change in style—somewhat, anyway—in order to compete with better teams in the Champions League. But at the same time, maybe it should just do what it does. Why follow Barcelona? It's an interesting question—one that might sequester coaches in backrooms during the off-season.

NEIL LENNON—A BRIEF COACHING PORTRAIT

Neil Lennon might not be around for long. He stepped in quite recently and took the position of interim coach for Celtic. He was born in 1971 in Northern Ireland and spent many years playing as a midfielder for various teams, including Leicester City, Celtic, and Nottingham Forest. He spent most of his playing time with Celtic, and he's triumphantly returned to lead the team, for now anyway. And, make no mistake, it's truly an honor to coach Celtic. His appointment might turn into a long-term position. Still, he's leading the best in the country, thanks in large part to Brendan Rodgers (who recently moved on), and things are only looking up.

KEY PLAYERS AND THEIR CHARACTERISTICS

Callum McGregor, Scott Brown, James Forrest, and Nir Bitton

Callum McGregor—who was born in 1993 in Scotland—finds his way around center midfield. So far, he's played in over 125 games for the green and white.

Scott Brown—the team captain—has over 330 games under his belt with Celtic, a staggering amount to date. He's been a regular presence for Scotland's national team as well. Speaking from a place of experience, Scott Brown has been the man to lead the troops forward whereby Celtic has achieved an amazing amount of league success recently.

James Forrest is a veteran midfielder for Celtic, one who's played 200 games to this point. He's knocked in quite a few goals as well; to date, he's gotten over 45, and more are sure to come. He was born in 1991, and he's not even hit 30 yet. With so much experience, he's sure to be an asset for the next five or so years, provided he can avoid injury.

Nir Bitton, who was born in 1991 and hails from Israel, is a center midfielder who has appeared in over 115 games for Celtic. He's a steady performer who keeps things tidy on defense. It's been veteran players like him who have brought Celtic a string of league titles of late.

Overall Player Rating:
Callum McGregor: 9
Scott Brown: 9
James Forrest: 8.9
Nir Bitton: 8.9

KEY PLAYER STATS

(Total career goals with this club)

	Games Played	**Goals**
Callum McGregor	129	22
Scott Brown	332	26
James Forrest	210	48
Nir Bitton	116	8

WHAT TO WATCH FOR ON TV—HOW MESSI, NEYMAR, RONALDO, AND OTHERS PLAY

The leaders in Scottish soccer will jump out to a quick start with a flurry of attacks down the wings. Celtic excels at getting the ball down field with numbers in the box, and this subsequently ups the ante with the opposing team. The result is usually a fast-paced affair with bodies moving forward, and defenses are frequently tested. It's an up-tempo style of play led by talented and experienced players, some of which include James Forrest, Ryan Christie, Jonny Hayes, Olivier Ntcham, Emilio Izaguirre, Kristoffer Ajer, Jozo Šimunović, Mikael Lustig, Callum McGregor, Scott Brown, and Odsonne Édouard (who will be counted on to put in more goals), and Nir Bitton. They're a lively bunch, and wins tend to follow.

WHAT ARE THEIR CHANCES OF WINNING THE LEAGUE TITLE THIS YEAR?

Very good. Celtic is the leader and will likely write another chapter in the history books.

Overall Team Ranking: 9.3

CSKA MOSCOW

Twitter: @PFCCSKA_en
Founded in 1911
Russian Premier League titles (formerly called the Soviet Top League): 13
Russian Cup (formerly known as the Soviet Cup): 12
European Cup and UEFA Champions League: 0
UEFA Super Cup: 0

Known For
Very passionate fans
Exciting games
Grigory Fedotov
Valentin Nikolayev
Vágner Love
Fedor Chalov
Mário Fernandes
Igor Akinfeev

A BRIEF TEAM HISTORY

PFC CSKA Moscow—founded in 1911—has won the league championship on numerous occasions, including 1946, 1947, 1948, 1950, 1951, 1970, 1991, 2003, 2005, 2006, 2012-13, 2013-14, and 2015-16.

During the Soviet era, CSKA Moscow did well in the Soviet Cup (which would eventually become known as the Russian Cup) in the 1940s and 50s. Then there was a lull until 1991, when the club held the trophy again. It would have to wait until the early 2000s before it got things going again, winning the Russian Cup multiple times in 2002, 2005, 2006, 2008, 2009, 2011, and 2013.

It's a club seeking a title in the UEFA Champions League. Such a quest might not occur in the next year or so, but the club has a strong fan base that's hoping for big results, and with a little work the Champions League trophy might be within reach.

FACTS ABOUT THEIR CITY

CSKA Moscow plays in VEB Arena which opened in 2016. The team also might hop over to Luzhniki Stadium for some games. Luzhniki Stadium was built in 1955 and kicked things off in 1956 as the Central Lenin Stadium (known as such from 1956-1992), named in honor of Vladimir Lenin, the first leader of the Soviet Union (who held office from 1922-24).

A few bars in Moscow for fans to enjoy a drink or two are Timeout Rooftop Bar, Bosco Bar, and Dream Bar.

WHERE THE TEAM IS TODAY—
TACTICS AND STRATEGIES

In 2018-19, CSKA Moscow was seen using a 3-4-3 a 3-5-2 and a 3-4-2-1 (the latter can be construed as a 3-4-3). Will it stray away from these formations? It's possible but not likely at this point. Most clubs tend to stay with a familiar routine, and CSKA Moscow will likely do the same throughout 2019-20. Though, if some formation tinkering occurs it wouldn't be surprising.

Tactics and strategies: keep the ball going to Fedor Chalov.

The young goal-scorer, Chalov, has proven to be a handful for the opposition. A continued effort to get him the ball in advantageous positions around the box would be wise. He's also a leader on the team with assists, so having the flow of play go through him should inevitably provide good touches on the ball for everyone. Obviously you can't use him in the attack every time, but, in essence, a steady diet of Chalov getting the ball should, in theory, be beneficial. In 2018-19, Chalov had help from Arnór Sigurdsson, Nikola Vlasic, Mário Fernandes, Ivan Oblyakov, and Rodrigo Becão, among others. With these players in place, assuming they don't get traded, good things should continue to build for CSKA Moscow and its young forward, Chalov, should continue tallying up goals.

VIKTOR GONCHARENKO—
A BRIEF COACHING PORTRAIT

Viktor Goncharenko was born in 1977 in the Soviet Union. He played as a defender with a couple teams, including FC RUOR

Minsk, based in Belarus. Now a few years have passed, and as coach of CSKA Moscow, Goncharenko has a mission that is to take the Russian Premier League championship, with an eye on making waves in the UEFA Champions League. Should he win Europe's highest club tournament, it would be the first for CSKA Moscow, thus creating a legendary place in club history for Goncharenko. Can he do it? Can he get there? It's possible. However, a Champions League trophy-lifting moment will have a lot of intense challenges along the way. He does, though, have an exuberant group of players on his side, and it should be a fascinating season.

KEY PLAYERS AND THEIR CHARACTERISTICS

Fedor Chalov, Arnór Sigurdsson, and Mário Fernandes

Fedor Chalov—or Fyodor Chalov—is a leading scorer for CSKA Moscow and also an assist provider. He's a league leader as well, one to keep an eye on if you're an opposing defense. He was born in 1998, and the young player already has a few games under his belt with Russia. He should be a valuable component to his club side for years to come. That is, if he isn't traded.

Arnór Sigurdsson is a young midfielder who was born in 1999 in Iceland. He brings a confidence and swagger that has been exuded by the new generation of soccer players from Iceland. He's been gaining a little experience with his national team, and he's definitely a player on the rise, proving his worth in the Russian Premier League.

Mário Fernandes was born in Brazil though he represents the Russian national team. He's also a standout midfielder and defender—one that specializes out wide—with CSKA Moscow; to date, he's played over 170 games; while no one will accuse him of being the biggest goal-scorer, he provides leverage for his team on the flank with speed, tenacity, and experience.

Overall Player Rating:
Fedor Chalov: 9
Arnór Sigurdsson: 8.9
Mário Fernandes: 8.9

KEY PLAYER STATS

(Total career goals with this club)

	Games Played	Goals
Fedor Chalov	60	24
Arnór Sigurdsson	17	4
Mário Fernandes	174	2

WHAT TO WATCH FOR ON TV—HOW MESSI, NEYMAR, RONALDO, AND OTHERS PLAY

The 2018-19 season saw some great performances from Fedor Chalov, Arnór Sigurdsson, Nikola Vlasic, Mário Fernandes, Igor Akinfeev, Ivan Oblyakov, and Rodrigo Becão. Many others played good supporting roles. Moscow was enchanted with excitement given the season's journey, and, not to mention, the 2018 World Cup. All that momentum is certainly spilling over to this 2019-20 season laid out for CSKA Moscow. The Russian Premier League is the playground, and a league championship will be on each player's mind. As 2019-20 rolls along, the team—which includes many Russian-born players—will be counted on for continued production, as the fans are eager for a spectacular year. Fedor Chalov and Arnór Sigurdsson should be at the top of the list for goal production, and if they can get going, it will likely affect others—such as Ivan Oblyakov, Arnór Sigurdsson, and Rodrigo Becão—in a positive way.

WHAT ARE THEIR CHANCES OF WINNING THE LEAGUE TITLE THIS YEAR?

Good, but it's not a given. There will be strong resistance from Zenit Saint Petersburg, Lokomotiv Moscow, FC Krasnodar, and, last but not least, Spartak Moscow.

Overall Team Ranking: 9.1

APPENDIX: OTHER EUROPEAN LEAGUES

These were the teams from 2018-19 season. The 2019-20 season should be an exciting one!

The Netherlands—Eredivisie
PSV Eindhoven
Ajax Amsterdam
Feyenoord Rotterdam
SC Heracles Almelo
AZ Alkmaar
VVV Venlo
Vitesse Arnhem
Excelsior
Willem II Tilburg
ADO Den Haag
Heerenveen
PEC Zwolle
De Graafschap
FC Emmen VV
Fortuna Sittard
FC Utrecht
FC Groningen
NAC Breda

Scotland—Scottish Premiership

Heart of Midlothian

Hibernian

Livingston

Kilmarnock

Celtic

Rangers

Aberdeen

St Johnstone

Hamilton Academical

Motherwell

St Mirren

Dundee

Norway—Eliteserien

Rosenborg

SK Brann

Molde

Haugesund

Ranheim

Odds BK

Valerenga

Kristiansund BK

Tromso

Sarpsborg FK

Bodo/Glimt

Stromsgodset

Lillestrom

IK Start

Stabaek

Sandefjord

Sweden—Allsvenskanliga
AIK
Hammarby
IFK Norrkoping
Malmo FF
Östersunds FK
BK Hacken
GIF Sundsvall
Djurgardens IF
Orebro SK
Kalmar FF
Elfsborg
IFK
Sirius
Brommapojkarna
Dalkurd FF
Trelleborgs FF

Denmark—SAS-Ligaen
FC Midtjylland
FC Copenhagen
AaB
AGF Aarhus
AC Horsens
FC Nordsjaelland
Esbjerg FB
Brøndby
Randers FC
Odense Boldklub
Sonderjyske
Vejle BK
Vendsyssel
Hobro IK

Austria—Austrian Bundesliga
FC Salzburg
St. Pölten
LASK Linz
Austria Vienna
RZ Pellets WAC
SK Sturm Graz
Rapid Vienna
SV Mattersburg
TSV Hartberg
FC Wacker Innsbruck
SC Rheindorf Altach
FC Admira Wacker Modling

Switzerland—Super League
Young Boys
FC Zürich
FC Basel
FC Thun
St Gallen
Lucerne
FC Sion
FC Lugano
Grasshoppers
Neuchatel Xamax

Hungary—Nemzeti Bajnokság I
Balmazújváros
Debrecen
Diósgyőr
Ferencváros
Haladás

Honvéd
Mezőkövesd
Paks
Puskás Akadémia
Újpest
Vasas
Videoton

Portugal—Portuguese Liga
Braga
FC Porto
Benfica
Sporting CP
Rio Ave
Maritimo
Santa Clara
Feirense
Guimaraes
GD Chaves
Moreirense
Belenenses
Tondela
Vitoria Setubal
Boavista
Desportivo Aves
Portimonense
CD Nacional de Madeira

Belgium—First Division A
Racing Genk
Club Brugge
Anderlecht

Antwerp
Standard Liege
Sint-Truidense
KAA Gent
KV Oostende
Cercle Brugge KSV
Royal Charleroi SC
KV Kortrijk
Eupen
Waasland-Beveren
KSC Lokeren
Zulte-Waregem
Mouscron

Greece—Greek Super League
PAOK Salonika
Atromitos
AEK Athens
Olympiakos
Aris
Panathinaikos
FC Xanthi
Panetolikos
Panionios
Larissa FC
Pas Giannina
Asteras Tripoli
Lamia
Levadiakos
OFI Crete
Apollon Smyrni

Bulgaria—First Professional Football League
Beroe Stara Zagora
Botev Plovdiv
Botev Vratsa
Cherno More Varna
CSKA Sofia
Dunav Ruse
SFC Etar Veliko Tarnovo
Levski Sofia
Lokomotiv Plovdiv
Ludogorets Razgrad
Septemvri Sofia
Slavia Sofia
FC Vereya
Vitosha Bistritsa

Romania—Romanian First Division
FCSB
CFR Cluj-Napoca
Gaz Metan
Viitorul Constanta
FK Astra Giurgiu
Universitatea Craiova
Sepsi Sfantu Gheorghe
Dunarea Calarasi
CSMS Iasi
Concordia Chiajna
FC Botosani
Dinamo Bucuresti
Hermannstadt
Voluntari

Russia—Russian Premier League
Zenit St Petersburg
Krasnodar
Rostov
CSKA Moscow
Spartak Moscow
FK Rubin Kazan
Lokomotiv Moscow
Ural Sverdlovsk Oblast
Gazovik Orenburg
Akhmat Grozny
Dinamo Moscow
Anzhi Makhachkala
FC Arsenal Tula
FC Ufa
Krylia Sovetov
Yenisey Krasnoyarsk

Ukraine—Ukrainian Premier League
Arsenal Kyiv
Chornomorets Odesa
Desna Chernihiv
Dynamo Kyiv
Karpaty Lviv
Lviv
Mariupol
Oleksandriya
Olimpik Donetsk
Shakhtar Donetsk
Vorskla Poltava
Zorya Luhansk

AUTHOR'S NOTE

All information in this book was up to date at the time of publication (July 2019). Every effort was made to stay on top of relevant information—such as goals scored and trades.

The goals scored by players will likely change over time. This stat reflects a good glimpse of the contributions from each player at the time this book was published. Keep in mind, books are not published one day before the season starts. Books, as opposed to newspapers, magazines, and online publications, do not have the luxury of updating stats on the fly. A stat like this will not remain constant since players usually play more games.

As for players being traded: Again, it wasn't possible to update last-minute trades or players being sidelined with injuries.

All player ratings in the "Overall Player Rating" sections were based on a scale of 10, just like gymnasts. This was a fun, yet tricky, part of the book. For instance, if Maradona were playing right now, he wouldn't be a 10, even though he's a 10. Same for Pele and other players deserving of a 10. So, for instance, at this current time, Messi might not be a complete 10, as he was in 2009, but he's still a 10. He's slowing down a little, yet, like Ronaldo, he recently won the Ballon d'Or. Messi is still arguably the best player in the world. Therefore, Messi is currently deserving of a 10 rating even though he's aging and reaching the point of not being a 10 at the highest level of competition any more. The same can be said of Ronaldo. They're still 10s, just not for long.

Any changes regarding players, coaches, and teams may potentially be updated on my website (shanestay.com) as well as others.

The top five teams in each section were not listed best to last. Let's just say, sometimes it's good to mix things up.

Concerning the teams from less prestigious leagues: Unfortunately, not all lesser known leagues from Europe were listed. As it turns out, of the less prestigious leagues, some are less prestigious than others. Of the leagues listed, some teams may have been relegated, or, in fact, gone bankrupt since the publication of this book. The latter is unlikely, but still a possibility. As of 2018-19, those teams listed were active. It should be said, though, that listing teams from less prestigious leagues creates awareness of their existance. Each of their respective leagues sometimes go unnoticed. When I was a kid, I subscribed to *Soccer Digest* (a magazine) and *Soccer America* (a newspaper). Both publications were dedicated to soccer primarily for an American audience. In *Soccer America*, there were lists of European leagues with the current standings. I was fascinated with all the teams, many of whom were new to me. I hope, for someone out there, listing these teams raised a certain level of curiosity as well.

Thanks to all the people behind the sources that were used in this book, including *ESPN*, *The New York Times*, and *The Washington Post*. Thanks also to Meyer & Meyer Sport, Cardinal Publishers Group, Melvin Parks, and Phil Greer.

END NOTES

1 Tariq Panja, *"U.S. Billionaire Gets Full Control of Arsenal, Buying Out Russian Rival,"* The New York Times, published August 7, 2018, accessed October 24, 2018, https://www. nytimes.com/2018/08/07/sports/soccer/arsenal-alisher-usmanov-stan-kroenke.html

2 Kevin Draper, *"A Rebuilt Liverpool Hopes to Reach New Heights With Its Soul Intact,"* The New York Times, published August 9, 2018, accessed October 24, 2018, https://www. nytimes.com/2018/08/09/sports/premier-league-liverpool.html

3 Joshua Robinson, "Manchester City: The Greatest Team in Premier League History?" *The Wall Street Journal*, published May 14, 2018, accessed November 1, 2018, https://www.wsj. com/articles/manchester-city-the-greatest-team-in-premier-league-history-1526324079

4 Ibid.

5 David M. Halbfinger, *"Roman Abramovich, After Visa Troubles in Britain, Surfaces in Israel,"* The New York Times, published May 28, 2018, accessed June 15, 2019, https://www.nytimes.com/2018/05/28/world/europe/roman-abramovich-israel.html

6 Roger Gonzalez, "Manchester City vs. Chelsea score: Kepa-Sarri battle steals the show before City captures trophy in penalty kicks," *CBS Sports*, published February 24, 2019, accessed February 25, 2019, https://www.cbssports.com/soccer/news/manchester-city-vs-chelsea-score-kepa-sarri-battle-steals-the-show-before-city-captures-trophy-in-penalty-kicks/

7 Rory Smith, "Maurizio Sarri: Chelsea's Tuscan Son," *The New York Times*, published August, 10, 2018, accessed December 14, 2018, https://www.nytimes.com/2018/08/10/sports/maurizio-sarri-chelsea.html?rref=collection%2Ftimestopic%2FChelsea%20Football%20Club&action=click&contentCollection=soccer&region=stream&module=stream_unit&version=latest&contentPlacement=3&pgtype=collection

8 Nick Britten, "10 things you didn't know about Wolverhampton," *The Telegraph*, published on December 31, 2009, accessed December 22, 2018, https://www.telegraph.co.uk/news/newstopics/howaboutthat/6911571/10-things-you-didnt-know-about-Wolverhampton.html

9 Ciaran Fahey|AP, "Bayern enduring its worst Bundesliga season in 7 years," *The Washington Post*, published February 4, 2019, accessed February 6, 2019, https://www.washingtonpost.com/sports/dcunited/bayern-enduring-its-worst-bundesliga-season-in-7-years/2019/02/04/e508ce10-2893-11e9-906e-9d55b6451eb4_story.html?noredirect=on&utm_term=.4a9c6508490d

10 Ibid.

11 Rory Smith, "We're Here! RB Leipzig's Rise to Bundesliga Isn't Welcomed by All," *The New York Times*, published August 26, 2016, accessed February 21, 2019, https://www.nytimes.com/2016/08/28/sports/soccer/bundesliga-rb-leipzig-red-bull.html

12 Ibid.

13 Ibid.

14 Ibid.

15 Ibid.

16 William Kennedy, "The Yellow Trolley Car in Barcelona, and Other Visions," *The Atlantic*, January 1973 Issue, accessed February 23, 2019, https://www.theatlantic.com/magazine/archive/1973/01/the-yellow-trolley-car-in-barcelona-and-other-visions/360848/

17 Daniel Alarcón, "The Superhero," *The New Yorker*, published April 22, 2015, accessed February 23, 2019, https://www.newyorker.com/sports/sporting-scene/lionel-messi-barcelona-superhero

18 Joseph Wilson | Associated Press, "La Liga Recap: Girona hold 10-man Barcelona to draw," *Los Angeles Times*, published September 23, 2018, accessed March 1, 2019, https://www.latimes.com/ct-90mins-la-liga-recap-ben-yedders-hat-trick-leads-sevillas-rout-of-levante-20180923-story.html

19 Mark Ogden, "Real Madrid's third straight Champions League title cements place in history," *ESPN*, published May 26, 2018, accessed February 26, 2019, http://www.espn.com/soccer/blog/the-match/60/post/3509636/real-madrids-third-straight-champions-league-title-cements-place-in-history

20 Charly Wilder, "36 Hours in Madrid," *The New York Times*, published September 21, 2017, accessed February 27, 2019, https://www.nytimes.com/interactive/2017/09/21/travel/what-to-do-36-hours-in-madrid-spain.html

21 Raphael Minder, *"Madrid Taxi Strike Intensifies After Barcelona Drivers Are Offered Concessions,"* The New York Times, published January 23, 2019, accessed March 3, 2019, https://www.nytimes.com/2019/01/23/world/europe/spain-taxi-strikes-uber.html

22 Lao-tzu, translated by Stephen Mitchell, *Tao Te Ching: A New English Version, with Foreword and Notes, by Stephen*

Mitchell, HarperCollins Publishers, Perennial Classics, New York, 1988, chapter 30.

23 *Wikipedia, The Free Encyclopedia*, s.v. "Seville," accessed March 4, 2019, https://en.wikipedia.org/wiki/Seville

24 By The New Yorker, "Video: Soleá, the Flamenco of Seville," The New Yorker, published November 11, 2014, accessed March 5, 2019, https://www.newyorker.com/culture/culture-desk/video-solea-flamenco-seville

25 Stephen Hawking, *The Theory of Everything: The Origin and Fate of the Universe*, New Millennium Press, Beverly Hills, California, 2002, p. 131.

26 Tom McGowan and Paul Gittings (CNN), "Villarreal give life ban to rogue fan who threw banana at Dani Alves," *CNN*, updated April 29, 2014, accessed March 14, 2019, http://edition.cnn.com/2014/04/28/sport/football/dani-alves-banana-racism-football/index.html

27 Ibid.

28 Alex Yannis, *"PLATINI IS SHOWING HIS BEST TO COSMOS,"* The New York Times, published August 12, 1984, accessed March 23, 2019, https://www.nytimes.com/1984/08/12/sports/platini-is-showing-his-best-to-cosmos.html

29 Ahiza Garcia, "Cristiano Ronaldo is the third athlete to sign Nike 'lifetime' deal," *CNN*, published November 9, 2016, accessed March 22, 2019, https://money.cnn.com/2016/11/09/news/companies/cristiano-ronaldo-nike-lifetime-contract/index.html

30 Ibid.

31 Kurt Badenhausen, "Why Cristiano Ronaldo's $1 Billion Nike Deal May Be A Bargain For Sportswear Giant," *Forbes*,

published Dec 2, 2016, accessed March 22, 2019, https://www.forbes.com/sites/kurtbadenhausen/2016/12/02/cristiano-ronaldos-1-billion-nike-deal-is-a-bargain-for-sportswear-giant/#1409bffb5a91

32 Rory Smith, "Ronaldo Joins Juventus, and Everybody Wins," *The New York Times*, published August 17, 2018, accessed February 26, 2019, https://www.nytimes.com/2018/08/17/sports/cristiano-ronaldo-juventus.html

33 Jeanne Bonner, "Return trip to Italy: You can recapture travel magic," *CNN*, updated October 2, 2017, accessed March 21, 2019, https://www.cnn.com/travel/article/return-trip-italy/index.html

34 Ibid.

35 James Masters, "Juventus beaten at Atletico to leave Ronaldo on brink of Champions League exit," *CNN*, updated February 21, 2019, accessed March 23, 2019, https://www.cnn.com/2019/02/20/football/champions-league-var-juventus-atletico-madrid-spt-intl/index.html

36 Ibid.

37 Tom Sunderland, "AC Milan Sack Coach Vincenzo Montella and Replace Him with Gennaro Gattuso," *Bleacher Report*, published November 27, 2017, accessed March 25, 2019, https://bleacherreport.com/articles/2736333-ac-milan-sack-coach-vincenzo-montella-and-replace-him-with-gennaro-gattuso

38 Rory Marsden, "Report: Arsene Wenger to Join AC Milan to Replace Gennaro Gattuso as Manager," *Bleacher Report*, published November 5, 2018, accessed March 25, 2019, https://bleacherreport.com/articles/2804595-report-arsene-wenger-to-join-ac-milan-to-replace-gennaro-gattuso-as-manager

39 Silvia Marchetti, "Starbucks in Milan: Is this the end for Italian coffee?" *CNN*, published September 7, 2018, accessed March 13, 2019, https://www.cnn.com/travel/article/starbucks-milan-italy/index.html

40 Daniella Matar|AP, "Milan players fight among themselves during loss to Inter," *The Washington Post*, published March 18, 2019, accessed March 30, 2019, https://www.washingtonpost.com/sports/dcunited/milan-players-fight-among-themselves-during-loss-to-inter/2019/03/18/146e2be6-498c-11e9-8cfc-2c5d0999c21e_story.html?noredirect=on&utm_term=.7de36d3e301b

41 Clint Henderson, "Milan: Italy's overlooked city is the crossroads of art, fashion and culture," *Fox News*, published July 13, 2017, last update September 27, 2017, accessed March 13, 2019, https://www.foxnews.com/travel/milan-italys-overlooked-city-is-the-crossroads-of-art-fashion-and-culture

42 John Brewin and Martin Williamson, "World Cup History: 1990," *ESPN*, published April 30, 2014, accessed March 28, 2019, http://www.espn.com/soccer/news/story/_/id/1834593/1990

43 Andrew Dampf|AP, "Spalletti calls Icardi's feud with Inter 'humiliating'," *The Washington Post*, published April 1, 2019, accessed April 1, 2019, https://www.washingtonpost.com/sports/dcunited/spalletti-calls-icardis-feud-with-inter-humiliating/2019/04/01/dff86ac4-5468-11e9-aa83-504f086bf5d6_story.html?noredirect=on&utm_term=.11d9b1c5527f

44 Gore Vidal, "In Fellini's Roma," *Vanity Fair*, published November 2006, accessed March 17, 2019, https://www.vanityfair.com/news/2006/11/fellini-in-rome-200611

45 Bija Knowles, "Visiting Rome? Insiders share tips," *CNN*, updated July 18, 2018, accessed March 18, 2019, https://www.cnn.com/travel/article/insider-guide-rome/index.html

46 Ibid.

47 Rory Smith, *"Film in His Blood, a Soccer Revolution in His Plans,"* The New York Times, published January 21, 2019, accessed April 4, 2019, https://www.nytimes.com/2019/01/21/sports/napoli-aurelio-de-laurentiis.html

48 Ibid.

49 John Sinnott, "Qatari takeover heralds new dawn for Paris Saint-Germain," *BBC Sport*, published August 3, 2011, accessed April 7, 2019, https://www.bbc.com/sport/football/14393012

50 Tim Lister, "The Qatar connection to soccer's record Neymar transfer," *CNN*, updated August 4, 2017, accessed April 7, 2019, https://www.cnn.com/2017/08/04/middleeast/neymar-qatar-connection/index.html

51 Ibid.

52 Ibid.

53 Vivienne Walt, "Kylian Mbappé Is the Future of Soccer," *TIME*, published October 10, 2018, accessed April 8, 2019, http://time.com/collection-post/5414056/kylian-mbappe-next-generation-leaders/

54 Corinne Labalme, *"WHAT'S DOING IN; Lille,"* The New York Times, published March 14, 2004, accessed April 10, 2019, https://www.nytimes.com/2004/03/14/travel/what-s-doing-in-lille.html

55 Jerome Pugmire | AP, "PSG again fails to seal French title after crushing 5-1 loss," *The Washington Post*, published April 14, 2019, accessed April 15, 2019, https://www.washingtonpost.com/pb/sports/dcunited/saint-etienne-beats-bordeaux-to-stay-in-chase-for-3rd-place/2019/04/14/b839f0b8-5ede-11e9-bf24-db4b9fb62aa2_story.html?nid=menu_nav_accessibilityforscreenreader&outputType=accessibility&utm_term=.c3839e0156d5

56 Rory Marsden, "3-Time Defending Champs Real Madrid Out of Champions League with Loss vs. Ajax," *Bleacher Report*, published March 5, 2019, accessed March 5, 2019, https://bleacherreport.com/articles/2823652-3-time-defending-champs-real-madrid-out-of-champions-league-with-loss-vs-ajax

57 *Wikipedia, The Free Encyclopedia*, s.v. "Heineken," accessed April 18, 2019, https://en.wikipedia.org/wiki/Heineken

58 James Masters, "Rod Stewart tells Celtic boss Brendan Rodgers: 'You've ruined my holiday'," *CNN*, updated February 27, 2019, accessed April 23, 2019, https://www.cnn.com/2019/02/26/football/celtic-brendan-rodgers-rod-stewart-spt-intl/index.html